LIPSERVICE: THE STORY OF TALK IN SCHOOLS

Open University Press

English, Language, and Education series

General Editor: Anthony Adams

Lecturer in Education, University of Cambridge

This series is concerned with all aspects of language in education from the primary school to the tertiary sector. Its authors are experienced educators who examine both principles and practice of English subject teaching and language across the curriculum in the context of current educational and societal developments.

TITLES IN THE SERIES

Computers and Literacy
Daniel Chandler and Stephen Marcus (eds.)

Children Talk About Books: Seeing Themselves as Readers
Donald Fry

The English Department in a Changing World
Richard Knott

Teaching Literature for Examinations
Robert Protherough

Developing Response to Fiction
Robert Protherough

Microcomputers and the Language Arts
Brent Robinson

The Quality of Writing
Andrew Wilkinson

The Writing of Writing
Andrew Wilkinson (ed.)

Literary Theory and English Teaching
Peter Griffith

Forthcoming

Developing Response to Poetry
Patrick Dias and Michael Hayhoe

The Primary Language Book
Peter Dougill and Richard Knott

Lipservice: The Story of Talk in Schools
Pat Jones

English Teaching from A–Z
Wayne Sawyer, Antony Adams and Ken Watson

In preparation

English Teaching: Programme and Policies
Anthony Adams and Esmor Jones

Collaboration and Writing
Morag Styles

LIPSERVICE: THE STORY OF TALK IN SCHOOLS

Reflections on the development of talk and
talk opportunities in schools 5–16

Pat Jones

Open University Press
Milton Keynes · Philadelphia

Open University Press
Open University Educational Enterprises Limited
12 Cofferidge Close
Stony Stratford
Milton Keynes MK11 1BY, England

and

242 Cherry Street
Philadelphia, PA 19106, USA

First published 1988

British Library Cataloguing in Publication Data

Jones, Pat
    Lipservice: the story of talk in
    schools: reflections on the development
    of talk and talk opportunities in schools
    5–16.
    1. Oral communication——Study and teaching
    I. Title
    401'.9   LB1572

    ISBN 0–335–15825–0

Library of Congress Cataloging in Publication Data
Jones, Pat, 1944–
    Lipservice: the story of talk in schools.

    Bibliography: p.
    Includes index.
    1. Communication in education.   2. Teacher–student
relationships.   3. Verbal behavior.   4. Classroom
environment.   5. English language—Study and teaching.
    I. Title.
    LB1033.J65   1988   371.1'022   87–34705

    ISBN 0–335–15825–0

Typeset by Butler & Tanner Ltd., Frome and London
Printed in Great Britain at the Alden Press, Oxford

For Pat D'Arcy who asked the difficult
questions and Julia who helped to
make my answers come clear.

Contents

General Editor's Introduction   ix

Part one: Setting the scene   1

   Introduction   3
1 **Snapshots**   5

Part two: Learning-talk: the theory   11

2 **Learning to talk**   13
3 **Talking to learn**   23

Part three: Learning-talk: the practice   31

4 **Learning-talk in action**   33
5 **Patterns of talk in schools**   51
6 **Bricks in the wall**   68

Part four: Finding the right context for talk   85

7 **Exploring the arenas**   87
8 **The nature of the task**   103
9 **The learning model**   111

Part five: Overview   127

10 **The changing context**   129
11 **Tearing down the wall**   141

Appendix 1 **The Groby Oracy Research Project**   159
Appendix 2 **Encouraging talk**   163
Appendix 3 **The implications of this book for oral work**   167
              and its assessment at 16+

References   175
Index   177

General editor's introduction

We are indebted to another major contributor to this series, Professor Andrew Wilkinson, for the coinage in the mid-1960s of the word 'oracy', on the analogy with 'literacy', so as to give legitimate significance to the role of talking and listening within the curriculum. Yet, at that time, as the then Certificate of Secondary Education (CSE) syllabuses in English clearly show, the talking that was taking place in English classrooms was of a very structured and formal kind — reading aloud, making prepared speeches, engaging in debates, and the like. The progression from 'oracy' to the more general use of the word 'talk' marks an important development: a recognition that less formal spoken language can make an important contribution to the learning process. Currently, we might say that we have made progress so far as talk is concerned but that we have been less successful in putting listening on the educational map. Indeed, my own (with Esmor Jones) recent (1987) publication *Now Hear This* (Oliver and Boyd) is one of the few textbooks for the classroom that actually seeks to help develop students' skills as listeners.

I have, therefore, to declare an interest in the classroom role of the spoken language, something that I have been concerned with since my days as a comprehensive school English department head. (One of my earliest publications was an article for the English Speaking Board's journal, *Spoken English*, on the role of free, unstructured talk in the classroom and this was later quoted in the chapter on the role of talk in the Bullock Report.) My worry at that time, as now, was the excessive formality of much that passes for talk in the classroom rather than allowing more scope for talk as simple interaction between students as people and learners.

The title of this book says a good deal. Over the last 20 years we have come to recognise the vital role of talk in the classroom, not just in the teaching of English but as an element in language work that covers the whole curriculum. The work of Douglas Barnes, amongst others, has been of central importance in alerting us to the relationship between talking and

g. Yet, in spite of the quantity of theoretical work in the area, there
en very little real change in the extent of productive talk that students
lly engage in during the teaching day.

Pat Jones's book explores this and analyses some of the reasons why it
should be so. More importantly, he suggests remedies and gives teachers,
not just of English, some clear pointers about how to improve their practice
in this respect. This is especially timely. As this introduction is written the
director of the National Oracy Project has just been appointed and the new
General Certificate of Secondary Education (GCSE) has been taught for
nearly a year in schools. This examination will ultimately place an importance upon the role of talk as a means of expression and examination across
a wide variety of subject areas and thus act as a further means of legitimising
talk in the classroom even more than at present. Sadly, even in the late
1980s, this is seen by many teachers (English teachers amongst them) as a
threat rather than an opportunity and there is certainly much uncertainty
about how to handle the volatile nature of classroom talk. Pat Jones's book,
based as it is upon successful teaching experience, classroom-based action
research, and sound theory, will make a major contribution to easing their
concerns. No extravagant claims are being made in the text; indeed as
General Editor of the series I felt that the author at times undervalued the
role of purely free talk in which students were free to chat during the
working day – something that adults in offices do all the time. The author
has provided us with a hard-headed account of what talk in the hands of
a sympathetic teacher can achieve and he is especially good on how to
create the conditions within which such talk can take place.

We know from a number of surveys that the young school-leaver needs
spoken English skills in the work-place much more than he or she needs
those of the written form. How to develop such skills and how they are
related to the remainder of the learning process is the subject-matter of
this book. It is the first in a series that we hope to publish about this
important, and still neglected, area of the curriculum.

Anthony Adams

There are only two lasting things we can leave our children –
one is wings, the other roots.

Richard Whitfield

PART ONE
Setting the scene

Introduction

> If you try to nail things down too much in the novel, you will either kill the novel, or the novel will get up and run away with the nail.
>
> D. H. Lawrence

This is not a book which sets out to provide definitive, formally researched findings about talk in schools. When beginning the book I spent several weeks struggling to create a satisfying framework, a coherent and logical structure for what was to be written. Every separate outline I produced only served to cramp the flow of ideas, to put things into compartments that never belonged there in the first place. If I was not careful I would be writing a book I did not want to write.

Instead, let me be clear about the limitations of this book and what it seeks to offer. I am writing above all about impressions formed from personal experience in a variety of schools for the last 20 years, from a two-teacher rural primary school (run by wife and husband) in the middle of a forest, through a girls' grammar school, to a number of relatively tough comprehensives. My own full-time teaching has been mainly in the last category, but two years' advisory work throughout Wiltshire and a year on an action-research project centred on one family of schools gave me a wider experience and broader perspectives.

What I have been increasingly interested in during that time is the role talk plays in learning and the use made of it in schools. Alongside other teachers in workshop and enquiry groups in Wiltshire and Leicestershire I have carried out a number of enquiries based on close observation. Most of those pieces of enquiry have had talk as their central concern.

Sometimes I feel that we teachers can overload a simple classroom incident with an unwieldy and unconvincing structure of meanings and generalisations. So when Wayne appears to be liberated by writing on computer paper rather than in his exercise book we tend to fly to the assumption that this new context for writing is relevant for all pupils. It may just have been that Wayne was in the right mood that day or that it was a good title. And other pupils might hate computer paper. In a profession where the borderline between success and failure is a fine one, you would be unwise to make a summer out of such a swallow.

This book tries to create its insights through a number of case studies viewed through a set of spectacles with a personal, customised tint. The significance of those insights is perhaps given more force when they are based on a number of case studies over a number of years and when some of those observations have been made closely and at times systematically. In other words, I believe that much of the experience referred to in this book adds up to something more coherent than a number of isolated incidents.

In this book I try to tell a number of stories; these stories are not fiction but, like good fiction, they try to point to the truth. As any worthwhile story surrenders more than one meaning, I invite you to share mine and to create your own. If common themes emerge then so much the better for their collective power. If you are not satisfied by them or not content with their meaning, then they are only stories.

So I do not set out to 'prove' things. To 'prove' things about schools you need at least a team of people working for an extended time in a variety of contexts. It has always amused me how enormous and painstaking efforts, such as the Rutter Report (1979), tend to come up with ideas which are at first hailed as the real truth and then increasingly challenged. The points that eventually emerge as agreed are ones that a good teacher or parent could have told you before they started: I am reminded by the £40,000 study which proved that children read more if they are surrounded by a rich choice of attractive books. No, 'proving' things it not something I am comfortable with, nor something which lies within the scope of this book. Instead let me be content with trying to present a number of materials, experiences and attendant insights that will support schools in their work, that will be of interest to thinking teachers and may offer them some routes to understanding what is happening in their own schools and classrooms. If the ideas in the book can help to create some new routes, or to rediscover some old ones then that would give me the greatest satisfaction. The ultimate test for the worth of any educational writing is that it should enable schools to become better places (just a little bit better) for young people to learn in. What else is more important?

Though this book may appear to be a solo effort there is a throng of people behind me as I write, people who have worked alongside me in classrooms and departments, people who have welcomed me in their schools and given me the benefit of their time and advice; people who have talked through things with me in small corners of staffrooms, on the windy spaces of long walks and in pubs with good beer (especially that). No need to name names; they know who they are. Above all, this book is populated by children: big ones, little ones, rowdy ones, placid ones, ones whom I have nearly hit and ones for whom love would not be too strong a word; ones whose names and faces have faded, ones whom I could not possibly forget. My debt is to them: they have been my teachers. Much of this book is taken up with examples of their talk; my stories are really their stories.

1 Snapshots

First moves

4S were the top stream in a grammar school in Nottingham. They took English literature a year early so that they could concentrate on German in the fifth year. I taught them in a top-storey classroom overlooking the slums of what was then the Meadows area, and the nearby secondary modern school. As my class dutifully and silently bent over their essays on 'First Impressions are Sometimes Wrong' or 'A Factory at Night', I grew bored and looked out of the window. My eye was drawn to some pieces of paper fluttering down from the top classroom of the adjacent school and to a cluster of youths half hanging out of the window. They could see me, too, and offered a mixture of friendly waves, vulgar gestures and catcalls in my direction. Behind them I could clearly see the teacher conducting the lesson as if nothing was happening. As I remember it, he was delivering what appeared to be a formal lecturette, with the odd scholarly reference to something on a blackboard behind him. In front of him were rows of empty desks. I took the staffroom copy of the *Times Educational Supplement* home with me that night.

Tutorball

The measure of your importance in a school hierarchy is whether you have an office or not. I was sitting in mine one day, rearranging the drawing pins on the notice board, when a knock came at the door. 'Come in!' I shouted, picking up a pen and shuffling some papers in front of me. In shambled Ray Porrit, who said to me: 'Sir says tutorball'. 'Pardon?' I said. 'What was that?' 'Sir said to come and see you and tell you tutorball.'

I was Ray's Year Head and I taught him English – or he had ended up in my class as he had been disruptive elsewhere. He seemed a nice, sensible lad – even a quiet lad, but he could not read and write. He attacked each piece of paper offered by writing his name with a flourish at the top and never anything more. By the age of 15 he was the father of two daughters (by different mothers) and so he had certain qualities and experiences which others in his peer group lacked. They admired him for this and Ray was proud about this achievement. One wonders what he would have made of it on the self-assessment section of a profile. But for the moment, this 'tutorball' thing intrigued me. I had to get to the bottom of it.

'Who is your teacher, Ray?'

'Don't know.'

'Ah! What's the subject?'

'Dunno.' (This after two terms.)

'Well you'd better take me there to find out what this is all about.'

Ray took me down the corridor to where a History lesson was in progress. A CSE set were reading a worksheet on battle machines and transferring it in a slightly altered form into their exercise books. Ray's empty desk (with its single sheet of clean paper) was at the back. As we came into the room the teacher greeted me with a slightly sheepish grin. He was a dynamic and forceful department head for whom I had a great deal of professional respect.

'Ah, Pat. Now Ray was behaving in a completely unacceptable way and refused to get on with his work after several warnings, so I told him to come and see you and tell you he was unteachable.'

Ray smiled: yes, that was the word.

The stuff that dreams are made of

Scene: a fourth-year Biology lesson. The teacher delivers a skilful lecture interposed with the odd closed question. He finishes and asks finally: 'Now, has anyone any questions?' A hand is raised towards the middle of the group; the teacher brightens.

'Yes?'

'Sir, why do we have to learn all this stuff?'

Turning the beer brown

I once taught General Science as a fill-in for a term. The course was a thoroughly prepared one for less able students and with a bit of mugging up I was able to keep at least one worksheet ahead of the class. The first one was on yeast and baking. Side one gave some simple facts about the topic:

> Most plants contain a green colouring called *chlorophyll*. This chlorophyll enables them to make their own food by *photosynthesis*.

It went on to note that yeast gives off *alcohol* when it respires.

The teacher talked it through. The class turned over and got on with the questions on the back.

1 The green colouring in plants is called c............
2 Plants make their own food by p............
3 The brewer uses yeast because it makes a............ when it respires. ....

Jane was halfway down the queue to get answers checked. When it came to her turn, sure enough she had got the answers right like all the others. Her correct answer to question (3) showed that she had absorbed the fact that the brewer uses yeast to make alcohol. I was beginning to feel a bit of an automaton doing all this checking and decided a quick chat would be nice and would help Jane to reinforce her learning.

'Can you explain to me in your own words why the brewer uses yeast then, Jane?'

Jane panicked, looked wildly round, went red and then blurted out with the unsure, rising tone of a question: 'Because it turns the beer brown, sir?'

Remember the albatross

The teacher began his introduction to the *Ancient Mariner* to his first-year class. He liked (he told me) to have some open, exploratory talk to raise the issues of the poem and introduce its main features before actually reading it with the class.

'Now can anyone tell me the name of a big bird?'

Hands shoot up.

'Carrion crow, sir?'

'Yes, that's quite big. Any more?'

'Pigeon?'

'Well, that's smaller than a crow. Anyone else?'

'Oo! I know, sir.'

'Yes, Jamie?'

'An eagle.'

'Well actually I was thinking of an albatross.'

Playing the right game

The following letters were exchanged between my seven-year-old son Sam and his friend Alan who had been his classmate in a 'sound' and traditionally-run primary school very popular with parents. Sam then moved with the family to a new county and a new school, where classes were team-taught in flexible bases, the work being organised through half-termly themes. All this was not very popular with parents, some of whom bussed their children to a school down the road which had uniform and setting for English and Maths.

Dear Sam

Thank you for your letter. It's great at .... School and we've already had a spelling test and we've done our times tables. Do you like your new school? Please write and tell me about it.

Alan

Dear Alan

Thank you for your letter. It's great at .... Primary School. We played a game called the Titanic ship and it sunck. The passengers got away in lifeboats but us the crew had to sink down with our ship for there was more than 100 of the crew and too many for the boats.

Love,
Sam

Dear Sam

Thank you for your letter. I wish I could play that game! It sounds good. At .... when you get one hundred stars you get a certificate, do you? I've got two stars already. We get mental arithmetic tests. In PE we have races and our team kept winning.

From,
Alan

Monday 4 February: three images

Stage 1

The teacher on early morning break duty walks through the playground like the Pied Piper surrounded by children, holding hands with two of them.

Stage 2

A teacher stands by the door as the third year troops into assembly, checking that everyone is dressed correctly. He has a supply of spare ties in his pocket.

Stage 3

An ugly-looking cluster of teenagers stands round the main entrance of the school jeering and banging to get in as the teacher padlocks and chains the double doors from the inside.

Removing the blocks

Devizes, April 1986. I had been invited by the Wiltshire/DES Oracy Project to talk to them about oracy in schools. For several days I had searched in vain for a metaphor that would illustrate and encapsulate my thinking about the issue of how talk develops in schools between the ages of five and 16. A short while before my session I went for a jog to clear my mind. Within yards of the conference centre I came across a magnificent flight of locks and interlocked basins that must once have been busy and flowing with life as the water and boats passed down the various stages. Alas, the locks had fallen into disrepair through disuse and the middle section seemed to be permanently shut, choked with weeds and silt. At the bottom of the flight a mechanical digger was at work. At great expense, and enormous trouble, the council were now trying to reopen this once thriving passageway.

I had found my image.

PART TWO

Learning-talk: the theory

2 Learning to talk

If we taught children to speak they'd never learn

William Hull

If it is true that all normal five-year-olds come to school with a vocabulary of several thousand words, enough basic control of grammatical structure and vocabulary to enable them to cope with the everyday demands of life, what do we teachers make of it? Can we assume that the development will continue naturally without our intervention or can we actively influence and encourage growth?

The balance of evidence as I perceive it falls inevitably in the middle. Children have the innate and developing capacity to acquire language but without a rich and varied context for its use, the growth of language will be stunted. So much is clear to me both from theoretical readings and my own observations as a teacher and parent. The work of Margaret Donaldson (1978) has been particularly helpful to me here in mediating between the theoretical ideas of Chomsky and Piaget and the common-sense view of everyday experience. In particular, I am attracted by the way she refuses to see the acquisition of language as something independent of other learning, or as something divorced from the everyday context of life. She concludes (p. 38): 'It is the child's ability to interpret situations which makes it possible for him, through the active process of hypothesis-testing and inference, to arrive at a knowledge of language.'

The Bill Hull quotation above is an attractive one which might on the surface seem to deny the power of the teacher to do little more than watch things happen. But if we all believe that schools and teachers are as irrelevant and impotent as he implies then the stories of our successes as teachers which sustain us can be dismissed as mere fiction. Let us pursue the Bill Hull idea a little further. Hull's one-time colleague, John Holt (1967, p. 57), muses:

Suppose we decided that we had to 'teach' children to speak. How would you go about it? First, some committee of experts would analyse speech and break it down into a number of separate speech skills. We would probably say that since speech is made up of sounds, a child must be taught to make all the sounds of his language before he can be taught to speak the language itself. Doubtless we would list these sounds, easiest and commonest ones first, harder and rarer ones next. Then we would begin to teach infants these sounds, working our way down the list ... When the child had learned to make all the sounds on the sound list, we would begin to teach him to combine the sounds into syllables. When he could say all the syllables on the syllable list, we would begin to teach him the words on our word list. At the same time we would teach him the rules of grammar, by means of which he could combine these newly-learned words into sentences. Everything would be planned, with nothing left to chance; there would be plenty of drill, review, and tests to make sure he had not forgotten anything.

Suppose we tried to do this; what would happen? What would happen, quite simply, is that most children, before they got very far would become baffled, discouraged, humiliated, and fearful, and would quit doing what we asked them.

It is a devastating fiction and we cannot deny its truth. What is wrong for children (and for teachers) is the learning model involved in such a process. One learns language by being in a situation that calls language forth. So we should take the focus away from language teaching and on to language learning. The teacher's job is to provide those rich and varied contexts that will enable language to grow rather than to set up sequences of artificial drills to inculcate language. Such sets of drills are often called 'courses'. The image that the word 'course' brings to my mind is one of a series of hurdles that we put in the way of competing racehorses only three of which win and some of which fall down early on. As Illich (1971) points out, the Latin derivation of 'curriculum' is a track round which slaves race for the pleasure of others.

But let us not be deceived that the provision of enabling contexts is something easy and effortless, however much the phrase trips off the tongue. I will argue later in this book in some detail that if such contexts are to operate successfully they require a great deal of careful thought and preparation within the framework of a very clear philosophy of learning and relationships.

Let me show you an example of the language that can grow from an enabling context. This particular story takes place in the privacy of the home, but is told every day in good infant classrooms.

Neil (aged seven) and Sam (aged five) enjoyed playing collaborative games with a big box of Lego. Whilst they played, the sustained bursts of chatter and laughter were accompanied by long silences as they raked the Lego to and fro in the box in search of particular pieces. One day they had been playing with my tape recorder. I was happy for them to do this, but had given them some guidelines, as good parents do: they were not to use my tapes (this after a tape I had been solemnly playing to an assembled body of teachers and other educationalists had suddenly been punctuated by two clicks, the word 'bum' and a bout of hysterical laughter); for safety purposes I had asked them to make sure it was unplugged after they had used it. The tape recorder was a portable one which would switch automatically to battery power if disconnected without being switched off. Once they had tired of replaying their collection of animal noises and inane giggles they unplugged the tape and continued their game. In this way a completely natural tape recording was made of two children talking together whilst they played. The following is one of several fascinating episodes from the tape. The game changed and developed continuously. The story of the part I transcribed is that there has been a crash and after the police and the mechanics have done their bit, the body of Zoomer is taken to a hospital where a very technical doctor diagnoses his problems. The play was centred around Lego figures, Smurfs and anything else that came to hand, including a plastic mouse.

1	*Sam:*	Pretend this car was crashed into a pole. We had to come to help, didn't we?
2	*Neil:*	Quick.
3	*Sam:*	Mend it, mend it.
4	*Neil:*	I take two persons.
5	*Sam:*	And I put, and I mend the car. It's brand new now.
6	*Neil:*	He's got to be whisked off to the hospital.
9	*Sam:*	Mine's got back. Park the car!
10	*Neil:*	He could be the one who crashed couldn't he?
11	*Sam:*	Yes.
12	*Neil:*	This one.
13	*Sam:*	Zoomer. He's called Zoomer.
14	*Neil:*	I goes in.
15	*Sam:*	I goes in. Hello!
16	*Neil:*	You puts your spanner down.
17	*Sam:*	I put it down, my spanner down there.
18	*Neil:*	Hang on I got to put ... I got to make the hospital a minute.
19	*Sam:*	What hospital?
20	*Neil:*	This! This is the hospital. (*Pause*) I got to attend to the patients sir ... You goes out again I'll check on the computer. I'll see if he's alright. He's not okay. He's got devices that shouldn't be in him. You says: 'Oh boy the scanner's gone on the blank'.
21	*Sam:*	Oh boy the scanner's gone on the blank.
22	*Neil:*	Uh-oh, what are we going to do?
23	*Sam:*	I don't really know.
24	*Neil:*	I'll see if this thing's working – I haven't even turned it on. (*Neil and Sam garbled*) It's not on the blank, it's not on the blank.
25	*Sam:*	I think I'll go out in my police car to see if there's any people crashed.
26	*Neil:*	Hey, this person's got German measles. He's got to be ... he's got to get to the doc ... the space doctor, cos he's from outa space.

You see we crashed. And your one's talking to the one in the red isn't he? Your one's talking to the one in the red. You see, we crashed and the spaceship collided with a pole – it went (*noise*). You see it crashed into.

27 *Sam:* It landed and it crashed.

28 *Neil:* It went (*noise*) and hit the post.

29 *Sam:* Pretend this was the spaceship. Alright Batman car the spaceship.

30 *Neil:* I've mended it. We needs a mechanic. See if I can make a mechanic. Oh yes this is the mechanic.

31 *Sam:* No it isn't – he squeaks, so he must be a mouse.

32 *Both:* A gigantic mouse!

During the game the boys switched in and out of roles naturally and spontaneously as the situation suggested. Neil seemed to take part in more role-play than Sam who was usually content to remain in the stance of the 'commentator' on his own actions. He does, however, take up a role on at least two occasions (5 and 25). This has implications for the language produced – but I will come to that later.

The tape itself contains a lot of expressive noises (groans, whines, half-sung bits of 'nonsense') punctuating the talk and at times slowly merging into talk. How does this fit into the whole language picture?

Much of the talk, too, contained a kind of utterance that is very difficult to classify, but which is contained in a lot of children's talk together. A typical example of this is 'You puts your spanner down' (16). Is this a command, a prediction, a statement of fact? In effect, I believe that it is a kind of collaborative planning of joint action – or a strong suggestion of how Neil wants the play to develop – and it is usually Neil who takes the lead. The extract contains at least 20 examples of this kind of talk which seems to me to be most interesting when considered as an aspect of children learning to share insights and situations, learning to work together rather than to obstruct each other. Neither's suggestions are refused or denied; they all change the nature of the game. There is no bidding or vying for the best idea, but a sharing atmosphere is built up. This is important for Sam. He is not the obvious leader of the play, but he feels free to participate and make his little suggestions (e.g., 1 and 29) in the secure knowledge that they will be adopted and made part of the game.

Neil seems to be very sensitive to the needs of the 'little boy' he is playing with, not only encouraging him by adopting his suggestions, but at times, perhaps consciously, teaching him words. Why else does he explain or reinforce the word 'collided' in 26, by the synonym 'crashed'? 'Collided' was not amongst Sam's current vocabulary; however he meets it not in isolation, but as part of an intensely realised and absorbing game, which has a visual context, too (Neil actually crashed the spaceship). The same is true of 'pole' (26) and 'post' (28). I asked Sam immediately afterwards whether he knew what the word 'collided' meant, but he did not. In July however, he did know 'crashed'. The seeds of the word had been sown in April and the next time he came across the word in context it was easier for him to recognise; soon it was 'his' word and part of his resources. He may misuse it at first (as Neil may have done with 'devices' (20)) but he will get it right soon enough. It seems to me that words and phrases are rarely built immediately into our vocabulary but grow in us until they become part of us. Perhaps they are more likely to grow in us when we are in the situation portrayed in the tape of two 'learners' talking naturally together sharing their vocabulary in context.

Throughout, Neil's vocabulary seems to me to be more sophisticated. Much of it appears when he is in role (e.g., 20) and when he is adopting what he takes to be the appropriate register for a highly technical physician. He has a phrase 'the scanner's gone on the blank' (20) which he may only half understand (he means 'blink', surely) and yet he is able to use it appropriately in context and he will in time get it perfectly right. (Note, too, how the seeds of this phrase are sown in Sam's head as he mechanically repeats the phrase at Neil's bidding.) 'Devices' (20) is used as a long, complicated word for dramatic effect. It sounds right and certainly fools Sam. Certain of the phrases in (20) are, however, correctly used social/technical jargon terms, which Neil has mastered and which, I contend, Sam was listening to in a very precise context. He was gradually building them into his consciousness: 'attend to the patients', 'check on the computer'.

Neil can also use register, tone and accent much more competently and fluently than Sam. He seems to have a 'model' in his head, quite possibly derived from a TV programme such as *Space 1999* which I know he watched. The mid-Atlantic accent which he adopts and which Sam really does have a go at in (23) is another clue here.

Most importantly, it seems to me that from this extract we can see patterns of language emerging through their casual encounter in purposeful conversation within a context of secure and warm relationships.

The tape of a discussion I had several years later with two seven-year-olds in school reinforced the impressions that the above tape had left with me and gave me some fascinating pointers as to how language is acquired. I was talking to Robert and his friend Mitchell about a story they had just told me together, based on a TV cartoon series called *He-Man and the Masters of the Universe*, which is a loose mixture of science fiction and fantasy, shot through with sexist attitudes. Robert and Mitchell loved it and had used its framework with a certain vigour and imagination in their own story. That is interesting in itself. Have such popular cartoons replaced spoken and literary stories in the culture of our homes?

Whatever the merits of the narrative itself I had been fascinated by the boys' confident, fluent use of technical terms and semi-technical language, some of which I was convinced was pure mumbo-jumbo to them. When they had finished telling me the story I talked to them about it.

Me: There are some things I didn't quite understand in the story. When you said 'force field projector', what's a 'force field'?

Robert: It's this thing that no one can get through it.

Me: What's a 'projector' then?

Mitchell: That means ... well it's this box thing that controls it, and if anybody blows that up, the force field would break.

(*Later*)

Mitchell: Skeletor is the one who's in charge of all of them. He's a right ... he's got a skeleton face ... And he's got this ... um ... he's got this Havoc Staff and it's got a round head on.

Me: He's got what?

Robert: A Havoc Staff.

Me: What's 'havoc' mean?

Robert: Don't know ... it causes havoc.

Me: What's that mean, 'causes havoc'?

Mitchell: It makes lots ... it makes lots and lots of trouble.

(*Later*)

Robert: He's just Prince Adam in the normal time and then he lifts up his sword and says 'By the power of Greyscar I have the power, ... and he turns into He-Man ... and then he goes like that to Cringer – that's his fearless friend – and then he turns into Battlecat.

Mitchell: Yes 'cos Cringer's really scared when he's in normal mode.

Me: What does that mean?

Mitchell: Well, it's um, like modes, like um ... just say ... um ... something transforms ... it's in like ... um ... let's say it transforms from a car to a robot. Then normal mode is robot, because it's mostly in that.

Me: What does 'cringes' mean?

Robert: He's really scared ... I think that's what it means.

(*Later*)

Me: What's a sorcerer?

Robert: It's a sorceress. Well it's this lady that's usually bad, but this one's very good.

Me: What do sorceresses do?

Robert: They make magic and things like that. And inside Castle Greyskull they've got this mirror called the mystic mirror and when someone causes trouble, she says 'Mystic mirror, all-seeing and all-heard ... this strange intruder to us now be shown'.

Me: This strange what?

Robert: Intruder.

Me: What's that mean?

Robert: It's um ... this traitor ... and ... um ... it shows the face.

Me: What's a 'traitor'?

Robert:	Um ... it's this person that says, 'I'll be your ... I'll be your slave' and he doesn't ... and he doesn't really.
Me:	Ah, right.
Robert:	My little brother called it a 'crater' ... a crater milk!!

My field notes made at the time read:

> This is fascinating. The regular watching of the programme seems to have slowly engraved certain features on his language. It would seem that the confident and accurate acquisition of the terms, so that they may be built into your store of language, is a slow, steady process. 'Traitor' for example began, presumably, as a meaningless word (like the little brother's 'crater milk' – simply a recognisable sound). It has now gained more accuracy. Robert has perceived that traitors don't always do what they say – though he can't generalise about this yet – he just gives an example from an episode he's watched. Robert is first aware of 'causes havoc' as a nice-sounding phrase, but he's beginning to link it with 'trouble'. Mitchell is well on the way to using 'cringes' confidently and accurately but he sees it largely as a symbol of fear, rather than a physical reaction. 'Intruder' and 'projector' clearly have some way to go yet, but as he encounters the words in different contexts (perhaps in this programme, perhaps not) and from different angles, he gets an increasingly accurate 'fix' on them until he uses them more or less accurately. We could say that he gets more numbers in the grid references and more cross-referencing to use with his language map. Throughout our life, if we are continuing and active language users, our 'fixes' on words get increasingly refined until, like the *My Word* participants on BBC Radio, we can make very subtle distinctions between words which on the surface share the same meaning.

There are whole strings of words used here with a degree of confidence one would not normally associate with seven-year-olds: 'Mystic mirror', 'fearless friend', 'normal mode', 'transforms from a car to a robot'. These are all directly attributable to the programme. Note, too, how he doesn't get all of it spot on yet: 'All-seeing and all-*heard*'.

It strikes me now that this is not so different to the way we adults continue to develop our language resources. We encounter new sets of language and begin to use them not necessarily with absolute accuracy. I once asked my ten-year-old son how it was that Dr Who's tardis was bigger on the inside. 'Oh,' he said, nonchalantly, 'it's spatially transcendental'. He would have picked up the phrase from the excellent Doctor, a past master at the art of the casual use of sophisticated jargon. I am reminded, too, of the colleague who advised me that if I wanted to do well at interview in a certain education authority, I would have to use the current 'buzz-words' which were 'modular frameworks' and 'active learning'. 'Doesn't matter that you don't know quite what you mean; they won't either,' he said, 'but they'll be impressed'.

I am using this particular tape as an example of one way that language seems to me to be acquired. I would not advocate that we should promote the linguistic development of children by exposing them to all the TV programmes they like and wait for it all to happen. Children undoubtedly do acquire language from such programmes but the process of education is more than just a matter of bolting bits and pieces of language on to unsuspecting bodies. I have grave reservations about the hidden messages contained within the particular programme referred to. The situations described are stultifyingly repetitious and ridden with emotional clichés. All is unacceptably subservient to dominant male power. Troubles are solved by swift and merciless violence. It seems to me that the moral and imaginative context within which the language is acquired is just as important and influential for the learner as the language itself. Articulacy is not the only yardstick by which we can judge the success of the learning process ... I have a number of present and former world leaders in mind. We can all think of people whose articulacy we admire but whom we would be ashamed to have taught.

Both the above encounters occurred in a sense spontaneously. Teachers must seek to open up such opportunities and make such spontaneity the stuff of the classroom. This is a matter of creating purposeful, non-restrictive frameworks within which talk flows naturally, with a little help from your friends and the teacher. An example follows.

A class of seven-year-olds were working on the theme 'robots'; all around me, robots were being made, painted, written about, experimented with. On a table in the middle of the room stood an inviting heap of Technical Lego and Capsella. A girl showed me a machine she had made. I asked her what it did and she said she did not quite know yet. From this spark grew an idea that provided a strand of classroom activity for a number of days; groups of children set about constructing their own 'marvellous machines' in preparation for an interview by their teacher and me in the role of 'roving reporters' from the BBC. The taped interviews were conducted very formally and these seven-year-olds rehearsed their ideas in very serious and professional voices. It was important that we were in role as reporters, but more importantly they were in role as the world experts on their machines; they were explaining something they knew about to an ignorant audience who needed to know. The children were 'in charge' and their language powers expanded to meet this new set of expectations.

BBC: Would you please explain to me about this weird-looking machine?
Keith: Well ... if I turn that, it will turn the chains, which will turn the wheel which will move it along ... Here I've got a seat with a few controls at the back. That's one of them and it sucks up all the dirt and grit on the roads and in the corner places. Just here is a fan to move it along which is also the engine.
BBC: What is it?
Keith: A self-propelled motor car.

(*Later*)

BBC: Can you think of a way of turning the fan round if this was on the road, belting along?

Keith: Well, if I put the control ... if I had a little battery connected on the bottom on the controls, then I'd ... I'd just have to switch it to 'on'. The fan would then turn round which would turn the chain which would keep the wheels moving.

BBC: Why do you suck the grit and dirt up?

Keith: Well, apart from being a self-propelled motor car, it is also a road sweeper.

BBC: Who are you hoping to sell this machine to?

Keith: The public.

BBC: What price?

Keith: (*Without hesitating*) Fifteen pounds 95 pence.

As an example of 'learning to talk' this repays scrutiny. Keith in one sense cannot be learning *about* anything. This is pure, unsullied fiction and he knows it. More importantly he is learning *how to do something*. He is flexing the muscles of newly-acquired language. The situation has elbowed him into a register which is unfamiliar to him, and which everyday contexts outside school do not often give him the chance to try (I guess). He is beginning to establish a tentative hold on a new language register which should eventually become part of his word-hoard. Note in particular his uneasy start, repeating a list of processes. As he gains in confidence, his language gains in ambition and fluency, so that the final three sentences of his first utterance have the control and ease of a skilled demonstrator: 'Just here is a fan to move it along which is also the engine.' The glorying in the phrase 'a self-propelled motor car' leads him to a compound sentence offered with complete fluency and competence: 'Well, apart from being a self-propelled motor car it is also a road sweeper.'

Children exposed to language will always acquire it to a greater or lesser extent. The teacher can speed up that process by the careful provision of opportunities within the classroom, and by ensuring that built into those opportunities are channels of communication through which talk – all kinds of talk – will flow. It seems to me that the basic questions teachers should ask about talk, at least at infant and junior level, are:

1 What kinds of talk should the children be exposed to, trying out and developing in their classroom?

2 How can I create opportunities for all these kinds of talk to happen?

Perhaps the best metaphor for the way I believe children learn to talk is that of a photograph slowly emerging from a developing tray: blurred, crude images at first, becoming increasingly clear and defined until one day, miraculously, we have a more or less complete picture – never perfect, sometimes out of focus, but the face of an individual shines through. As parents and teachers we cannot witness the continuous development of these features, any more than we can see flowers actually grow; but periodic glances out of the window reveal first shoots, then stems, then buds in a series of 'snapshots'. To quote from a talk given by Andrew Wilkinson at an NATE conference: 'Language obviously develops, but it doesn't develop obviously'.

So far I have tried to suggest that children learn to talk by being placed in contexts to which the natural response is language. The child will steadily accumulate language into his or her word-hoard ready for future unlocking when exposed to its purposeful use in contexts which give an outline of its shape and a series of clues about its meaning.

If that is my story of learning to talk then the rest of this book is about the use the learner can and does make of this more-or-less developed talking ability to make sense of the world: talking to learn.

3 Talking to learn

I had intended to write a chapter in this book which would painstakingly summarise how the case for a central role for talk in schools has developed over the last 20 years; to that end I spent the best part of three months reading what educationalists in the field judged to be the most influential books on talk written during that time. In the event, though the reading provides an indispensable background to this book, and though it confirms all I say, I did not judge it to be necessary or even valuable to make such an explicit historical survey here. And anyway, before I came to knock in this particular nail, the book had already come along and run away with it. For the books and publications I read revealed to me a powerful consensus about the centrality of talk to learning; indeed it proved most difficult to discover lasting and authoritative dissident voices on the subject, though I do quote Stuart Froome's dissenting voice from the Bullock Report. If teachers have even an outline sympathy with a tiny part of the writing I encountered, then to make the case for talk here would be to be preaching to the converted. Instead I have tried below to offer a selection of interesting quotations from the cannons of writing about talk simply to demonstrate that an articulate and ultimately moving consensus exists.

> There is no gift like the gift of speech; and the level at which people have learned to use it determines the level of companionship and the level at which their life is lived.
> This matter of communication affects all aspects of social and intellectual growth. There is a gulf between those who have, and the many who have not, sufficient command of words to be able to listen and discuss rationally; to express ideas and feelings clearly; and even to have any ideas at all. We simply do not know how many people are frustrated in their lives by the inability ever to express themselves adequately; or how many never develop intellectually because they lack the words with which to think and reason (DES 1963).

I speak ... in order to emerge into reality, in order to add myself to nature (Gusdorf 1965).

Pupils, like adults, need to talk over new experiences, returning to them again and again, maybe finding new elements and connections. The potential meaning of an experience ... is not always clear at once. It needs to be worked over, 'realized' again through language, shared and modified ... Talking it over, thinking it over ... can be natural parts of taking account of new experience (Dixon 1967).

It is not enough for pupils to imitate the forms of teachers' language as if they were models to be copied; it is only when they 'try it out' in reciprocal exchanges so that they modify the way they use language to organize reality that they are able to find new functions for language in thinking and feeling (Barnes *et al.* 1969).

We are saying that it is as talkers, questioners, arguers, gossips, chatterboxes, that our pupils do much of their most important learning. Their everyday talking voices are the most subtle and versatile means they possess for making sense of others, including their teachers. School should be a place in which we can hear the full sound of 'the conversation of mankind' (Barnes *et al.* 1969).

Discovering comes in seeing the meaning of what is new in terms of what is familiar; in his talk he creates for the new a personal context; nobody else can do it for him because it has got to be in relation to his own experience. And he does that, above all, in his talk (Britton 1970a).

Thus, it is above all in expressive speech that we get to know one another, each offering his unique identity and (at our best) offering and accepting both what is common and what differentiates us (Britton 1970b).

[The child] cannot talk without learning something about the content of the talk, for this is the goal of the communicators (Tough 1973).

Talking that is relevant to his experience may ... provide the child with a meaning for the experience different from that which it would have had if it had happened without the accompanying talk (Tough 1973).

It is a confusion of everyday thought that we tend to regard 'knowledge' as something that exists independently of someone who knows. 'What is known' must in fact be brought to life afresh within every 'knower' by his own efforts. To bring knowledge into being is a formulating process and language is its ordinary means, whether in speaking or writing or the inner monologue of thought. Once it is understood that talking and writing are means to learning, those more obvious truths that we learn also from other people by listening and reading will take on a further meaning and fall into a proper perspective (DES 1975).

We welcome the growth in oral language in recent years, for we cannot emphasise too strongly our conviction of its importance in the education of the children ... its essential place in preparing a child for reading, its function as an instrument of learning and thinking, its role in social and emotional development. In today's society talk is taking on an ever-growing significance. People are surrounded by words which are playing upon issues that will affect their lives in a variety of ways ... In recent years many schools have gone a very long way to asserting this aspect of education as one of their most important responsibilities. But there is still a great deal to be done. A priority objective for all schools is a commitment to the speech needs of their pupils and a serious study of the role of oral language in learning (DES 1975).

I would question the notion ... that a child can learn by talking and writing as certainly as he can by listening and reading ... It is doubtful if children's talk in school does much to improve their knowledge, for free discussion as a learning procedure at any age is notoriously unproductive ... I believe the Committee is in error in putting undue emphasis upon talking as a means of learning language. It has its place, but in my view, one of the causes of the decline in English standards today is the recent drift in schools away from the written to the spoken word (Froome 1975, pp. 558–9).

The major means by which children in our schools formulate knowledge and relate it to their own purposes and view of the world are speech and writing.
   I call this groping towards a meaning 'exploratory talk' ... It is usually marked by frequent hesitations, re-phrasings, false starts and changes of direction. I want to argue that it is very important whenever we want the learner to take an active part in learning, and to bring what he learns into interaction with that view of the world on which his actions are based. That is, such exploratory talk is one means by which the assimilation and accommodation of new knowledge to the old is carried out (Barnes 1976).

One of the major functions of language that concerns teachers is its use for learning: for trying to put new ideas into words, for testing out one's thinking on other people, for fitting together new ideas with old ones ... which all need to be done to bring about new understanding (NATE 1976).

... a school ... should be an environment in which all kinds of talk do in fact ... happen; where children can talk to adults in both formal and informal situations, where purposive, or directed talk goes on – as it always has – and where undirected and unconstrained conversations are also seen as part of the educative process ... ordinary talk has an important part to play in the assimilation of new knowledge and new experience; and ... we need to use our own particular everyday speech to do this.
   New knowledge has to be fitted in to existing knowledge, to be translated into terms of one's own experience and re-interpreted, and in this process (which can be called learning) thought and language are very close together. If any of it is to be made coherent and communicative, a ready-to-hand language is needed to net and give initial shape to the transient flow of ideas, perceptions, images, feelings. One's everyday speech is the nearest-to-hand language that everyone has and is therefore particularly appropriate for new learning situations (Martin *et al.* 1976).

In discussions with teachers and with heads, it was clear that at the centre of many difficulties and differences of view there lies a confusion between two functions of language – the first as as communication of what has been learned and the second of part of the activity of learning itself. Concentration on the first of these at the expense of the second, which is often more important, may obscure the stages of misunderstanding, approximation and correction through which the learner often needs to pass and also may reduce the pupils' engagement with learning ... A change of emphasis from language as evidence of learning achieved to language used in the process of learning is needed.

... [Pupils] need more experience as participants in genuine discussion, in which they attend to the contribution of others, learn to discriminate between the relevant and the irrelevant and to expand, qualify and range in and around a subject (DES 1979).

Talk offers teachers the most important means of promoting children's learning and a major means through which the aims of education can be carried out (Tough 1979).

The skills of using language are not developed in isolation from other learning but are part of, and essential to, all the learning we intend that children should achieve in school ... Talk contributes most to children's learning when it is based on the children's own direct experiences. Talk is an important dimension of children's experiences and largely determines the view that they will take of the world around them and the kinds of meanings they will develop (Tough 1979).

There is now a sizeable body of evidence to support the prime importance of language, and particularly talk, in learning. For the student who wants to succeed not only in understanding the broader problems of living through the twentieth century, but also in the more immediate task of passing examinations, there is no substitute for the understanding that grows from free and informal conversation with fellow students and teachers. The open school should buzz regularly with the exploratory talk of a learning community (Watts 1980).

If they are to extend their powers of language, children must be brought into contact with new experiences and ideas or look afresh at old experiences through discussion (DES 1980).

The primacy of the spoken word in human intercourse cannot be too strongly emphasised. Important though the written word is, most communication takes place in speech; and those who do not listen with attention and cannot speak with clarity, articulateness and confidence are at a disadvantage in almost every aspect of their personal, social and working lives (DES 1982).

Talking things through is an essential method by which we all make sense of our experience from earliest childhood, through school and on to adulthood. In school, children are given a lot to learn. One of the best ways of really learning and understanding something is to talk about it. Children's mental grasps of ideas, facts or opinions develop as they try to express what they mean, or listen and respond to other people (Richmond 1983).

What schools should provide, therefore, is the opportunity to develop and extend these conversational skills by putting them to use in the exploration of the new ideas and experiences that the more formal curriculum provides (Wells 1984).

A fuller understanding of the nature of linguistic interaction, whether at home or in the classroom, is leading us to recognize that, to be most effective, the relationship between teacher and learner must, at every stage of development, be collaborative (Wells 1985).

All children, we would argue, will learn most effectively when there are frequent opportunities for collaborative talk with teachers and with fellow pupils (Wells 1985).

To achieve some objectives, for example mastering the skills of analysis and constructing a reasoned argument, it will be necessary for pupils to talk through a problem, to try out hypotheses or conduct a personal experiment ... It is necessary to ensure that pupils are given sufficient first-hand experience, accompanied by discussion, upon which to base abstract ideas and generalizations (DES 1985c).

Through listening and talking in groups children are enabled to explore other people's experiences and to modify and extend their own ... All pupils need to be given ample opportunity for discussion of a wide range of experiences (DES 1985c).

Pupils should be encouraged to explore ideas which are new to them in their own words before being introduced to the technical terms for those ideas (DES 1985c).

Pupil talk in a lesson has many functions. It increases the understanding of concepts, enables pupils to learn how to communicate clearly with others, makes them active learners, gives them a diversity of viewpoints and a critical tolerance of others.

The most important reason for encouraging pupil talk is that it will increase the pupils' understanding of scientific concepts. Concepts are embodied in language, even in our thoughts. Our ideas are built up of words and phrases that make sense to us; other people's words and phrases may be remembered, but rarely, and it is our own reworking and collecting together of words and examples that help us define and therefore understand concepts ... for most pupils most of the time this exploration will be done only through talk. If we do not provide the opportunity for our pupils to talk through concepts then the chances of them thinking them through at all, never mind successfully, is remote (Bulman 1985).

It is likely that pupils' performances could be substantially improved if they were given regular opportunities in the classroom to use their speaking and listening skills over a range of purposes in a relaxed atmosphere ... There is also evidence from research that gains made in mastery of spoken language may have beneficial effects on pupils' learning capabilities. The experience of expressing and shaping ideas through talk as well as writing and of collaborating to discuss problems or topics, helps to develop a critical and exploratory attitude towards knowledge and concepts (APU 1986).

These voices in a sense speak as one. Notes of dissent sound irregularly, feebly and without credibility. There is no passing bandwaggon inviting teachers to step on and move along a station or two. Bandwaggons are temporary affairs enjoying brief and overinflated popularity. Ultimately bandwaggons go away. The monument to the value of talk has been erected with more loving care and thought than any passing phase or craze. It has deep and lasting roots in linguistics, philosophy, theories of child development, sociology and in other strands of educational thought. It has stood the test of time. I chose the word 'monument' with care, denoting as it does something permanent, visible, perhaps with many names on, but not something living. Twenty years in and around schools have given me the strong feeling that the messages so clearly emanating from this existing body of thought about talk have never really got through in any radical sense to influence everyday classroom experience, though I believe that the majority of teachers accept them or pay lipservice to them. Like the sculpture of Ozymandias in Shelley's poem the monument to talk stands well carved, impressive, but around it the lone and level sands of barren classroom experience stretch far away. 'Look on my works ye mighty and despair.'

In the face of such a contrast between idea and reality the questions which had originally occurred to me as the important ones to ask when considering talk in schools began to change. I became less interested in discovering what the role of talk in learning was and more concerned with exploring the reasons that such a powerful consensus had not, within a 20-year period, been translated into radical changes in classroom practice. If I could understand that then perhaps I could go some way towards offering some ways forward what would mediate between the high ground of educational theory and the more mundane practical realities within schools and classrooms. In case the above broad analysis seems rather too sweeping and simplistic, let me add that on taking a closer look at schools and classrooms I found that there *were* dark corners, well-manured beds, whole allotments where talk was flowering and where teachers were busy planting seeds.

But before that part of the story is presented, perhaps I could offer the following brief summary of the case for using talk in schools. This began with an inspiringly simple summary given in an excellent booklet edited by Richmond (1983), the outcome of a day conference of 230 English teachers. These ideas were modified by a number of teachers from a variety of subject disciplines and age ranges within the family of schools I worked in during 1985–6. Below is the rationale for talk presented by those teachers as part of a longer policy document about talk in their schools (published in full in Appendix 2).

1 Talk is a potent natural means of learning, but in schools it tends to be overshadowed in importance by writing and reading.

2 To talk something through with others is an important way to grasp new ideas, understand concepts and to clarify your own feelings and perceptions about something.

3 A high proportion of classroom activity involves talk of two kinds: the teacher explaining while the pupils listen and answer the odd closed question; and pupils chattering in a non-purposeful way. This is not always disruptive, but neither is it fruitful.

4 It is important to encourage a more varied range of pupil talk in the classroom where, for example, pupils have the opportunities to discuss ideas at length; explain concepts; describe; narrate; speculate; reason; instruct; work together on common tasks and problems; role-play.

5 Natural opportunities for such talk occur in a variety of subjects, activities and stages. The development of talk is therefore the responsibility of all teachers.

6 In adult life and in the world of work talk is far more important than reading or writing and makes increasingly complex demands on individuals. If schools neglect talk they will not only deny young people a vital means of learning but they will be failing to equip them for life.

These fundamental beliefs inform the whole of this book.

PART THREE

Learning-talk: the practice

4 Learning-talk in action

Language in the classroom should be an instrument of learning not of teaching.

James Britton

The beliefs stated at the end of the last chapter need to be illuminated by examples of fruitful learning-talk which should lead us to a closer and more practical definition of what such talk looks like and what it can do. Along the way a number of issues will be aired.

The story-tellers

Nigel was seven, had lost most of his front teeth, and though he did not resent writing, found it just a bit of a struggle. Here is a typical example from his 'journal' in which he was encouraged to write in all kinds of ways from jotting ideas to complete stories:

> The Bot Family.
>
> one day Ted Bot and Mummy went to The wit Family. Ted Bot played with Kate wit. They went up stairs. Luke wit was Sleeping on The landing. Kate wit Woke him up Ted Bot was Still and Then it was time four Ted Bot to go home.
>
> The end

Well, he writes in sentences, and spells pretty well, but you would not make any grand claims for the imaginative quality of this piece. A positive view might stress the achievement of a complete, controlled narrative. A cynic might lament the impoverished development of anything but the mundane and superficial. All in all an unremarkable piece, typical of Nigel's efforts at story-making so far and bearing comparison with the efforts of a number of his peers.

One afternoon I was watching Sarah paint a picture. Great sweeps of green paint indicated two hills which framed the distinctive black outline of a castle from which protruded what appeared to be a gigantic chicken. Dark, lowering clouds from which grey streaks emerged indicated rain. Nigel, in-between doing things, sidled by.

'What are you painting?'

'I dunno,' replied Sarah casually.

This reply intrigued Nigel and he began to point out features of the painting which suggested a story. At my suggestion he then began to tell, on the wing, the story of the painting, as follows.

> One day there was a king that lived in a castle and he decided he would go out for a walk, so he went and got his big fur coat on, took his crown off, got his big winter hat on and went out. Just as he was getting into the carriage, he was blown over by the wind. So he got back, and he decided he didn't want to go on ... and then he lived happily ever after.

Already there is a development here from the example of his writing (completed a matter of days earlier). This is not just a matter of the somewhat livelier narrative progression and the less shallow exploration of meaning. What is most interesting to me is his use of ambitiously complex sentences within a literary style. The punctuation is all there in his delivery and intonation. Note particularly the confident progression of the first sentence and the tendency to inversion in the second. Here is no story in the spoken, fireside tradition. Before me was a written story told orally.

But Sarah was a much more demanding critic than I and not too pleased. 'You didn't say anything about the weather-cock [so *that's* what that gigantic chicken was] and it was raining in the picture.'

'Shall I tell it again?' asked Nigel, plaintively. And a second version emerged straight from head and tongue to tape recorder:

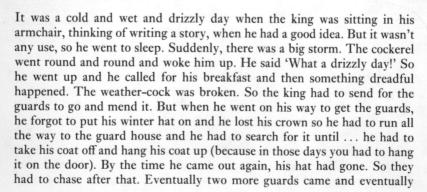

> It was a cold and wet and drizzly day when the king was sitting in his armchair, thinking of writing a story, when he had a good idea. But it wasn't any use, so he went to sleep. Suddenly, there was a big storm. The cockerel went round and round and woke him up. He said 'What a drizzly day!' So he went up and he called for his breakfast and then something dreadful happened. The weather-cock was broken. So the king had to send for the guards to go and mend it. But when he went on his way to get the guards, he forgot to put his winter hat on and he lost his crown so he had to run all the way to the guard house and he had to search for it until ... he had to take his coat off and hang his coat up (because in those days you had to hang it on the door). By the time he came out again, his hat had gone. So they had to chase after that. Eventually two more guards came and eventually

caught them ... and they went back to the castle and had some supper and they lived happily ever after.

Again I could judge the punctuation by his pace and tone. At the end of each sentence his voice dropped down and he paused to take breath and stock. Though he tends to begin many sentences with 'so' and 'but', they are really only ritual link words offered as pauses to enable him to take stock, think ahead whilst maintaining a narrative flow. In other ways there is a fine variety in his sentence length and construction. I particularly like the confident control of the first sentence with its unusual structure. I am sure that in writing he would omit the 'when' in his first line and use two separate sentences. In writing he appears to only be able to think in short, manageable blocks. When telling the story the tongue follows his thoughts and in a sense creates them as he goes along, whereas his pencil lags behind. There is a sense here of his pushing out the language boat, not sure of where it is going to land. As Sarah said when talking about story-telling: 'It's exciting – you can just think up things with your head and just blurt them out when you want to.'

The two versions of the story showed me something I had never encountered before in schools – that it was possible, indeed desirable, to *draft* stories orally. There has been a strong emphasis on written drafting in the last ten years, but I had always assumed that an oral story was something that emerged like a mayfly and then went away. Given supportive criticism, it seems that children are capable of 'redrafting' stories orally and indeed are keen to do so as there is less labour involved. A number of possibilities present themselves: children story-telling in small groups, commenting on initial versions, refining them and then telling a 'best' version on tape; children telling the same story from different angles – or producing their own individual fully-fleshed ideas from a skeleton outline presented. I suspect that a very fruitful area for talk and learning opens up before us.

Nigel's self-image as a story-teller grew by leaps and bounds from this point – to a stage eventually where he went a little too far and insisted on pinning people down in corners of the classroom and telling them long, rambling episodic stories with no end. But below is an example of his most outstanding achievement. It was told three days after his original king story and within ten days of his 'Bot Family' written story.

One day there was a robot and he came down from space in his spacecraft ... and he saw a fairground and he went over and he had a go on a roundabout, then the creaky stairs and he went on the creaky stairs to ... and there was this place where you had a horrible face and when you looked in the mirror behind it, it was a nice face .... so when the robot went in ... um ... he had a scare, because there was a horrible monster with a horn sticking in somebody's body. So he jumped up and down and he ran back out and he told the fair ... keeper; so they went in together ... and when they got there it was out ... so ... so ... so he decided he wouldn't go on that any more. So he went ... he went on the big wheel. He had fun on that. He could hear all the people ... and there was a big bonfire. Somebody saw the robot and decided to put him on the fire, and the robot said 'No, no, no, no, no, no, no! Don't put me on the fire! I've only just come out of the sky! I only wanted to have a go on the things.'

'No ... you are going on the fire', said the keeper.

'I'm not!'

'Yes, you are!'

And then he went on the water slide and when he got down and he got out, he had a walk about to get dry ... and then he rusted.

'Oh dear,' said the children, 'our favourite friend has been rusted. Who could have dared to go on that slide like a robot like him?'

'I don't know', said a little boy called Peter.

So Peter said to the robot, 'Would you like to come home with me and I'll clean you up and have you for my friend?'

'Yes, please', said the robot.

So Peter picked him up and took him home ... And then, he cleaned him up and they played on the beach – but he didn't dare to go in the water, so he made sandcastles and the robot buried Peter ... and then it was the robot's turn to be buried ... And then he jumped out ... He could see his friends in the ro ... in ... in ... in a ... machine up in the sky, so ... he shouted 'I'm not coming back home any more! I'm staying here!' So he stayed there in Australia and they lived happily ever after together.

During the first part of the story he is experimenting with ideas, rambling a little according to where his tongue takes him, though there are some imaginative ideas seemingly well beyond the author of the 'Bot Family'.

The story really takes off and achieves a narrative and imaginative coherence from the moment the robot encounters the bonfire. Until then it has consisted of a series of loosely-connected episodes told in a relatively detached way. Now Nigel enters into the imaginative world of the story. The dialogue begins to have life. Having been menaced by the bonfire-watchers, the robot is threatened by destruction from the rust and is saved by the small boy who befriends him and lovingly restores him. The robot has thus joined the human world and has lost his alien strangeness (which had presumably been the source of the earlier threats) to the extent that he can now confidently shed his former existence. In an important sense Nigel has created and shaped a story 'on the wing' without all the pencil-chewing labour and thinking-through one associates with the writing of a seven-year-old. I do accept that older, more fluent writers can achieve this organic spontaneity in creative writing but I am sure that for this particular seven-year-old the medium of talk is the only one that can channel, give shape and life to the meanings locked up in his head.

The development in Nigel's language is interesting, too. He now sees himself as a story-teller and feels confident in control; an expert, almost. Note the control of the short sentence 'He had fun on that'; the expressive plaintiveness of the robot's appeal to the menacing crowd: 'I've only just come out of the sky'. I find it surprising too that the 'literary' style of the story is maintained. Here is little of the relaxed, colloquial casualness of the oral story. He is telling a story in the style he has read to him at home and at school. So he does not say 'Peter said, "I don't know"', but '"I don't know", said a little boy called Peter'. He can hear his voice as he says this, and so slips easily into the narrative register, a blueprint for which exists in his consciousness.

Nigel's classroom adapted and developed to accommodate current interests and concerns. This was the conscious policy of his teacher. His story-telling activities sparked off a number of others anxious to have a go and tell a story to me, fresh out of their heads. On one unforgettable occasion a girl sat with me in a corner of this busy classroom, alive with voices, and began her story. Gradually as the story unfolded, children nearby stopped what they were doing and began to listen. Slowly the classroom hum stilled to silence and during the last few minutes, the girl sat on her chair surrounded by a dozen or so children sitting at her feet looking up at her, transfixed by her story.

I began to wonder what might emerge when spoken stories were written down; would the new dimension that had opened up for the children now be taken through in a written version? Would the rehearsal through the medium of talk carry over into their writing? The one thing I did not want to do was to force the issue and tell the children to write their spoken stories as that could no doubt prejudice their attitude to what they were doing and hence affect the product. I suggested to them that some of these would make good stories for their journals but no one took up the invitation directly. During the same period I did obtain one piece of evidence which gave me some clear pointers about the relationship between spoken and written work.

Some children had been taking part in an extended role-play with me. In their home-made time-and-space machine they had been visiting different eras and planets, inevitably coming across me when they got there as a medieval peasant, cave man, famous king or strange alien. In the extract below they are explaining to me about religion and the story of Jesus (for I knew nothing about their strange culture).

Alien:	Who was this man Jesus?
Annette:	Well, he was this man and he was Mary's . . .
Beth:	Mary's baby boy . . .
Annette:	Well, he was . . .
Nick:	Baby . . . they christened him, he was a baby . . .
Annette:	Well, when it was nearly Christmas . . .
Beth:	Day . . .

Annette: Christ ... no Christmas Eve ...
Nick: It was Christmas Day ...
  (*Indistinct*)
Annette: It was Christmas Day when he was born ...
Beth: Yes ...
Annette: It was nearly Christmas and Mary and Joseph ... these two ladies ... um a man and a lady.
Beth: ... and a woman.
Annette: And ... and ... they were expecting a baby and on Christmas Day they had this baby ... and God spoke to them and said ... um ... it would be called Jesus.
Beth: 'Call your ... '
Annette: 'Baby, "Jesus"' ... and they called their baby Jesus and when he grew up he was ... um ... a helpful boy and he could do magic ...
Beth: And he was hung ... by two nails in his hands.
Annette: Yes ... hands and feet.
Beth: And two nails in his feet that went right through his body.
Alien: But why if he was a helpful boy?
Beth: These people thought that he was a ...
Annette: was a bad boy ...
Beth: an enemy ...
Annette: an enemy ... but ... so they hung him up and um ... and it didn't look very nice ... um ... They put him in a grave ...
Beth: No it was in this cave, wasn't it?
Annette: Yes ... in this cave.
Beth: And they put this great big boulder ...
Annette: Yes ... but then he rose again ... he came alive again ... and then he ...
Beth: and he pushed the boulder away.
Annette: He pushed the boulder away and he came out again. And Mary, his mother, said 'How did you get out of there?' And she didn't know he had been alive all the time.

This is just a small section of a wide-ranging discussion which took up nearly a morning in-between bouts of space and time travel. In the afternoon Annette announced to me she was going to write about the morning's adventure. I asked her if she would like to write it to me, the alien, so I had something to take back with me. The alien had been very interested in the story of Jesus and so Annette began with that. Here it is, exactly as she wrote it.

About Jesus

Long long ago there lived a lady called mary and a man called josev. mary was about to have a baby. It was christmas eve, on Chirstmas day the baby was bron and god had told mary to gave the name Jesus to there baby. When he had grow up some pepol think his was a bad man so they high him up with nails in his hands and his feots, and high him up after that they put him in a graf.

We can make an interesting comparison here with Annette's share of the oral version. The written story was undertaken voluntarily and with some enthusiasm. I do not think Annette saw it as drudgery or indeed as 'work' in any conventional sense; it was simply something she wanted to do for half an hour.

The written version has the attraction of neatness and economy of narrative. Whole areas of the story are missed out or implied; so we have to assume that Mary had obeyed God's request about the name. I do not find the bare bones of this written version as attractive as the spoken version and believe that, were one to judge Annette's verbal ability from it, one would be seriously underestimating her capabilities. Purely judging by the sophistication of the language, it seems that she has exchanged some of her most ambitious phrases for less telling ones. So 'expecting a baby' becomes 'was about to have a baby', the idea of Jesus being able to 'do magic' and being 'an enemy' becomes simply that he 'was a bad boy', and God 'spoke to them' translates to the balder, less atmospheric 'told'. Because she cannot sustain the details in the written version, the whole thing has a more detached, less involved air. Nowhere is the commitment to the story as strong as in the spoken 'two nails in his feet, that went right through his body'. The emotions of the spoken version ('it didn't look very nice', the surprise of Mary, for example) are completely lacking as are several important details which flesh out the story and give it life: the boulder; the cave; Mary's words.

In short, I would assert that Annette's powers of language, imagination and narrative sense seem to emerge more fully in her spoken version. If this is accepted, what are we to make of it? The live audience was no doubt important, as was the collaborative nature of the story. Beth and Nick both support and contribute at important moments. It is difficult if not impossible to create in the written form the motivation that flows from this live, participative context. Yet one would assume that the ideas and language generated would overspill into the written version and might even emerge in a fuller, more controlled way, given the time for thought, reflection and shaping that Annette had. In fact very little is carried over. The comparison between the two stories offers a challenge, for this age-range at least, to the conventional notion that teachers have that talk is a useful 'foreplay' for the pre-writing stage.

Instead, judging by Annette's work, one is tempted to view the spoken version as something full, valid and complete in itself, and the writing as something subsidiary and different. It is almost as if Annette has two distinct 'modes' which she switches between. In the written mode she is more cautious, cramped and less developed. In speech she uses the (easily-spelled) word 'feet' unhesitatingly. In writing she experiments with 'foots', and 'feot' before settling for 'feots'. Her powers of language are dampened and subdued by writing in the same way that Nigel's were in the Robot story.

Later that week I tape-recorded a discussion between several children who had been involved in oral story-telling:

Eleanor: I think it's really good. It's exciting – and you can think up the things with your head. You can just blurt them out when you want to and then stop . . .

Beth: And you don't have to write it all down.

Eleanor: Sometimes when I'm kind of doing this story . . . I go 'oh yeah and then I'll do that and then I'll do this' . . . but I don't have enough time to write it down. I'm really itching to get it out and then I can't write it down quick enough. It's much much better doing it on tape.

Annette: You don't have to read things, you just get them from the top of your head, not from the book or anywhere . . . I think it's really good.

Nigel: You think of it – really want to get it down on your book and just as you go to plan it's just playtime and you have to go out straight away. When you get back it's not there anymore, so you have to think of something else.

Beth: I'm good at telling stories, but I'm not that good at writing them . . . because I get most of the words wrong . . .

Nigel: Making stories on tape is OK because you don't have to write anything down . . . When you're doing your own [written] story it takes a long time and you want to finish it . . . you want to go on to the last page . . . but you can't . . . you just want to do a whole page but you can't feel it coming . . .

Some obvious points come through here. The talking enables them to say more, and more quickly, and bypasses any technical problems with spellings. However enlightened the classroom, it seems that children will settle for less ambitious, more easily-spelt words in writing. Eleanor speaks of the attraction of the speed with which thought can be translated to language in oral sessions. What I find most fascinating is Nigel's hint at the end, that because of the labour of writing, the ideas that feed it are not actually formed and do not emerge – the channel is blocked by a barrier of written language and so 'he can't feel it coming'.

I believe, then, that in their oral story-telling the children are talking in a way that is fruitful for their learning. Their powers of language are being developed in a much more muscular and complex way. The imagination can operate without hindrance and hence the meanings they shape with that language are fuller and more complex. Children's powers of language and thought are more likely to develop at the frontiers of their ability – at the blurred interface of 'can do' and 'can't do'.

The medium of talk encourages them to explore this boundary. In writing not only are the boundaries less far-flung, but the children are more likely to settle for the cosy garden close by instead of the unknown wilderness on the horizon.

The candle alarm clock

The seven-year-old story-tellers were in a sense both liberated, and challenged, by the medium of talk. In the extract below a group of 12-year-olds are working together on a piece of science. Because it is science I shall focus in my subsequent analysis on the ways that the talk contributes to learning from the point of view of the scientist. From a wider perspective both the following extract and the ones of the story-tellers illustrate the development of the capacity to think, to imagine, and to use language to shape and give expression to those activities.

The four 12-year-old boys in this extract from a 40-minute tape had been given the following items of equipment from which they had to construct a kind of alarm clock, which they could make to 'go off' in half an hour: a milk-bottle; a fork; a tin; a candle; a length of thread; Plasticine; a split-pin or clip. They had already constructed a device depending on the clip being placed half-an-hour's burning time below the top of the candle. A thread was tied to the pin and subsequently onto the fork which was dangling in the milk-bottle. The teacher had commented that though the fork would drop in time, the noise produced was not loud enough to ensure that it would rouse a heavy sleeper.

During this extract the boys were experimenting with ways of producing more noise. Eventually they constructed a device whereby the fork was dangling over the tin from a thread which ran from the clip and over the top of the bottle to gain height. They decided to give this device a preliminary test, inserting the pin just below the top of the candle and at one stage speeding the pilot experiment by slanting the candle. The pilot worked, as is shown at the end of the transcript, and the boys went on to do the final experiment successfully (during their breaktime).

In the transcript neither I, nor the teacher, nor the pupils themselves were able to identify with confidence who the individual speakers were – hence the numbering. The difficulty in extricating individual voices from this dense and urgent mass of thinking-talk is in a sense a tribute to the success of its corporate quality.

1 Perhaps we could get the milk-bottle to fall on the tin.
2 Yeah. That's what I was thinking but it might smash.
3 Yeah. That's true. We wouldn't want to buy a milk-bottle every day.
4 Anyway, what do you want a fork for?
5 Oh, yeah. That's a point. You've got to use all the stuff.
6 (*Teacher*) Have you *got* to use all the stuff?

7 I think so, yeah.

8 What I thought was, when that falls down, if we had one of those foil forks it could come up and fall into there.

9 I reckon that's it.

10 Hey listen! Vibrations ...

11 I know, but that ... it's not as ... look if we can pull that out a bit more cos it'll burn slowly and that will come out slowly and that will (*interrupted by* 'if it hits the milk-bottle we're making a lot of vibrations ...') just hit there slowly.

12 That will fall out.

13 (*Teacher*) That's one thing you ought to find out. Will that paperclip come out suddenly?

14 Yeah it will.

15 Or slowly.

16 (*Teacher*) Why?

20 Because ... um ... the candle burns slowly and probably wax will melt around that ... and then ... that wax has got to burn for that to be able to come out ... see ... so um ...

21 Shall we tie it to a pin?

22 (*Teacher*) Are you saying that that fork's going to be slowly lowered onto the tin? What do you think?

23 I'm not sure.

24 Maybe we need a higher ... I reckon there's enough ... I reckon we need it a bit higher ... same here ...

25 (*Teacher*) Well, what do you think about that?

26 (*Indistinct*) We've got to find out how that will come out.

27 Hey! Hold on ... if you take that out ... like that ... and put that there, that's how it would fall.

28 But it's still got that ...

29 (*Teacher*) What you've got to think about is whether that's going to come out slowly or suddenly.

30 If we take it out and push it around so we can bend it round the candle, then it'll ...

31 No ... if you take that out a bit more, 'cos you said push it right in. If we take it out until it's about two millimetres in there, it should come out alright.

32 Yeah (*indistinct*).

33 (*Teacher*)You could try an experiment. I don't know whether Mr H—— would let you light the candles at this stage. Try an experiment right near the top.

34 They've got theirs alight.

35 Right ... stick it in just near the top ... right.

36 I'll go and ask him.

37 Will it hold (*indistinct*)?

38 OK. Leave it, Ash, leave it ...
    (*Boys set up the apparatus for the pilot experiment.*)

39 (*Teacher*) OK. This isn't the real thing, is it? This is an experiment to see how it comes out ... Then you'll measure ...

40 Measure it again (*indistinct*).
41 Keep it on there ... now keep it on there until it lights.
42 That's it ...
43 Stop it ...
44 The thing is you know that that's resting on there.
45 Yeah but ... (*indistinct*) and it burns for half an hour or is this just an experiment?
46 No, it'll only burn for about ... four minutes, till that wax is starting, then it'll go down, down, fall on the tin and make a noise.
47 Oh it's hitting the tin now, is it?
48 It'll first fall on the tin then ...
49 I dunno ... I dunno if it'll work or not.
50 Take one of these out.
51 Yeah you'll have to keep it out.
52 What about a pin ... put a pin in.
53 I shouldn't breathe too much on the candle. It might go out.
54 Just try it, see if it works. Might work.
55 Just the same as (*indistinct*).
56 It's melting quite fast.
57 Yes the two centimetres should be about ...
58 We should be [putting] – that over here.
59 I thought a pin would be better ... Yeah if we put that over there, then that will be higher and then it would go down and make a horrible noise.
60 Yeah, I know, but then the thread would burn.
61 Really we need the fork right up here, now, don't we?
62 Move the candle back a bit.
63 We could.
64 It's not really melting that side, is it?
65 Look it's going.
66 Yeah ... now it's tipped up ...
67 We can *make* it tilt, can't we?
68 Yeah ... we could have it wedged under there.
69 Yeah. But then it won't burn for half an hour will it? It'll burn quicker.
70 It'll burn a lot quicker then.
71 One side will burn ...
72 We could make the clip a bit further down ...
73 Yeah, we could always slant it.
74 We should make it slanted.
75 Yeah I know, but it won't burn so quick, will it? It burns quicker.
76 Yeah, but we could move it back, look.
77 (... but how do you know? ... *indistinct*).
78 Clip looks like it's moving ... clip's starting to come out. You can tell it's melting around it.
79 Should make a clash.
80 I dunno. Might come out too slowly, like Franny said.
81 If we could bend that wick over to that side ... get it straight, then it will balance ... (*indistinct*).

82 We *should* do it with a pin really instead of that.

83 No ... but ... you wouldn't be able to tie the cotton ...

84 Yes you would.

85 Yes you would, because it's the same as tying a fishing hook.

86 Look.

87 No, but that's got a hole.

88 You've got this bit ... a little cap. You could tie it onto there quite easily.

89 It's not burning that side.

90 It's gone up ... look at the way it's gone up.

91 Yeah, it's leaning this way.

92 That's going to break off some of that wax ... that pin.

93 It's coming now, because it's breaking off.

94 It's coming.

95 Yeah ...

96 Yeah, I reckon it will go suddenly.

97 Not suddenly ... sort of go a little bit, then ... but we won't recognise it because then ...

98 If we had the form higher (Yeah that's what I was thinking) then if it came out slow, give it more time.

99 Yeah (*indistinct*).

100 (*Teacher*) One interesting thing is that it pulls a ridge of wax up, doesn't it? (Yeah) And that's going to melt quickly, isn't it?

101 (*Indistinct – commenting on the movement of the clip.*)

102 Any second. It's going to go any second.

103 Here it goes. I can see it.

104 It's coming.

105 Yeah. It's coming out.

106 Yeah.

107 Oh ... look at that it's just in there.

108 How far? Who put it in?

109 (*Teacher*) The thing is, does it make a big enough noise when it comes ...

110 Yeah, 'cos I think we need it farther. (Yeah) if we can get it right up here ...

111 I think ... It's coming ... Don't touch it ... here we go ... this is just an experiment.

112 The fork here's just balancing on the top ... just balancing on the top.

113 Look, the pin's coming through there.

114 Yeah, you can see it the pin ... it's going to go any minute now.

115 *Second* not minute.

116 Yeah ... you can see it ... moving.

117 And the weight of the fork pulls it.

118 Yeah ... look at the fork moving! (*The fork falls onto the tin with a clang.*)

119 Bloody hell! That scared me!

120 It worked!

The first and most obvious feature of the discussion is its sustained involvement – no frivolous comments disturb the sustained absorption in a chunk of intense scientific activity. The key to this high level of involvement lies in the nature of the activity itself, the expectations of the teacher and consequently the self-image of the group. They see themselves as mini-scientists, as an independent group of learners in pursuit of a challenging and purposeful goal. The task raised the self-perceived status of the children's own thinking. Yet the goal was not to find the 'right' answer, to unlock what was in the teacher's head; for this was a genuinely open task. There were dozens of possible solutions and the group was intent on finding its own way through the plethora of possibilities opening up before them. The task was purposeful and highly focused; the piles of miscellaneous objects were immediately intriguing, tangible, beckoning and as the children huddled over them it became clear that this was a genuine group exploration.

The dialogue has a supportive, sharing tone about it; the children are co-operating in a common task. Comments are chipped in as they grope towards a common solution (30–32). Nobody's ideas are crushed or dismissed; hunches are followed through, taken up, or tactfully laid aside in the flow of thinking (58–60). It would appear from the tape that a social context for thinking is enormously valuable – as we have all experienced when we have tried out ideas in a supportive group, or when we have used another person as a sounding-board for half-formed, uncertain thoughts. The excitement and stimulus of a social situation can, it appears, generate thinking and the result of such co-operative thinking can be one that was initially beyond the capability of each of the individuals involved.

Throughout the tape it is possible to identify a variety of significant scientific processes at work and it is the developing quality of thought involved in this activity which is surely the justification for this kind of open-ended group work in schools. To begin with the children had to contemplate the objects in front of them and using logic and imagination, form a theory as to how these objects could be translated into a machine that would perform a given task. This stage of the task encouraged a deal of speculation, evident for example in (20, 46, 96). Calling on reservoirs of knowledge from past experience enables the group to cut corners, to avoid going down potentially unprofitable sidelines. For example, in (1–3), the idea of using a milk-bottle as the object dropped is dismissed before disaster happens. Once the experiment is under way some of the most involved parts of the tape show the children observing events very closely (78, 112) and speculation is renewed and adapted in the light of what is happening (92, 98). In (114–15) the skills of estimation are shown being exercised – based again on close observation.

The teacher's role at first sight appears to be that of the interested spectator whose attempts to prompt and guide are overlooked by the group.

However a closer look at the tape shows that his comments (29) about the speed of the lowering of the fork, though apparently ignored, are returned to at the end of the experiment (96). For most of the tape the teacher is content to take a back seat, to leave the learners in peace to find their own solution.

Final testimony to their intense engagement on this piece of scientific work comes at the end of this extract. The practical work of the Science lessons of my own schooling generally involved the repetition of an experiment, previously demonstrated by the teacher to achieve a pre-determined result. Rarely did I or my fellow pupils respond in quite the spontaneous way that this group did at the climax of their efforts: 'Bloody hell! That scared me! ... It worked!'

At the frontier of feeling

The evidence of the talk in the above extract shows that the four boys are closely involved in and committed to their work. Nevertheless there is still an element of clinical detachment in the talk and in the processes rehearsed. It would be fair to say that they are developing their thinking – exercising their minds. In the next extract, four girls in free discussion of the topic of handicapped children seem to be exploring the frontiers of their own feelings and in doing so are discovering as much about themselves as they are about the topic. The tape was made by a group of 15-year-olds who had worked together in this way on several previous occasions. They had in this way already worked through any tensions or difficulties and had achieved a good, secure working relationship. They were part of a fifth-year Humanities group to whom I had regularly offered the option of making a tape of group discussion as part of a number of suggested activities based on the topic we were currently exploring in the classroom. This is the final five minutes of a 20-minute tape.

1 *Anne:* Would you be able to look after a handicapped child ...?
2 *Mandy:* No, I think it'd probably get you down.
3 *Jane:* I'd probably need some help.
4 *Anne:* Probably yeah you'd need some help, but do you think you'd be able to cope with looking after one?
5 *Jane:* I would ...
6 *Mandy:* Did you see that programme ...
7 *Jane:* ... if they showed me what to do ...
8 *Mandy:* ... last year, where he went and got all them little things for the kids; that really upset me to think that he tried to do, them things and he hurt himself, you know what I mean?
9 *Sue:* That, that programme we watched last year?
10 *Jane:* Yeah, he had no legs.
11 *Mandy:* Oh ...
12 *Sue:* Yeah and no arms.

13 *Jane:*   Yeah. Yeah. But he had the good side about it didn' he?

14 *Sue:*   He did ...

15 *Anne:*   He got a chance to live.

16 *Mandy:* Yeah, I wasn't meaning not having his legs on. That's all right ... it's what ... it's when they just don't understand you.

17 *Sue:*   At least he's got a good brain ...

18 *Mandy:* Yeah, but that's what I mean; if they haven't got a good brain that's when I would do it.

19 *Anne:*   I know, but I think I'd be able to look after a physically handicapped ...

20 *Jane:*   ... You've got to be in the situation first of all, ain't ya? You've got to be in the situation.

21 *Anne:*   Yeah. It's probably different when you ... you're faced ... you've had this baby and you been waiting for it to be born for nine months ...

22 *Jane:*   ... just think all that ... all that pain and that ...

23 *Anne:*   ... then you suddenly have the baby and the doctor comes up and says 'Oh, it's handicapped'.

24 *Sue:*   It'd be horrible.

25 *Jane:*   I wouldn't disown it.

26 *Anne:*   I would ... I don't think ... I think it all depends if you're in that ... if you're depressed ... if you were in a depression he might do/like he might say ...

27 *Mandy:* Have you got bum ache? (*Jane was shuffling in her chair!*)

28 *Anne:*   ... he might say 'just get' ... might say 'get rid of it'. I mean he might just get rid of it.

29 *Jane:*   Yeah. But some doctors, though'd think it ...

30 *Anne:*   Yeah but some want it later on don't they?

31 *Mandy:* I know this woman –

32 *Jane:*   Shut up ... (*laughter*)

33 *Anne:*   I think it is rotten.

34 *Mandy:* Don't hit me ...

35 *Jane:*   I will if I want to.

36 *Mandy:* Don't be silly ...

37 *Jane:*   You know them doctors ... some doctors are taking the babies away from the mums without saying ... I don't think that that's right.

38 *Anne:*   No.

39 *Mandy:* I reckon it's ...

40 *Anne:*   I reckon every mother ought to have a choice.

41 *Jane:*   Yeah, because sometimes the doctors do though, don't they? In certain circumstances?

42 *Mandy:* I reckon it's a bit hard when a woman falls down and she hurts herself and she has to lose the baby – when she falls downstairs or something.

43 *Jane:*   Bet that's really mean.

44 *Anne:*   Yeah I know but ...

45 *Jane:*   Mind you if you lost your baby or summat and then you got all

them baby things to remind you of . . .

46 *Anne:* Oh yeah it'd be horrible.

47 *Mandy:* A miscarriage – someone across the road she had a miscarriage

48 *Jane:* 'Cos this woman . . .

49 *Mandy:* . . . and in the end she had to have another one/she had a miscarriage and then she could have the next one.

50 *Anne:* This woman I know, she was . . . she was ever so nice . . . Mary her name is. She's only young and she had this baby and it was blind . . . and dumb . . .

51 *Mandy:* Ahh!

52 *Anne:* . . . and it couldn't hear and it was there and she had to feed it by tubes and it was really bad you know and they kept it in this hou . . . er this sort of hospital thing at Woodhouse Eaves and they fetched it home for the weekend . . . and they had to sit up all night with her 'cos they named her and christened her and everything – all these pretty doll's clothes and everything – it was gorgeous . . .

53 *Sue:* Oh . . .

54 *Mandy:* I know. Don't it make you sad? And er . . . And they brought her home at weekends and they used to have to sit up all night with her and take it in turns to feed her . . .

55 *Jane:* Yeah but I bet it was worth it though . . .

56 *Anne* . . . but they put the tube . . . they had to put the tube up her nose and um Mary she put the tube up her nose and she seen all these tears come down the baby's face 'cos it'd hurt her and it couldn't make a noise to tell.

57 *Sue:* Ah . . .

58 *Mandy:* Ah . . . (*starts to cry*).

59 *Anne:* . . . and then it died . . . see it died . . . it couldn't cope any more . . . just died . . . so she's having another one now 'cos she says um/I feel better for having that baby.

60 *Mandy:* I feel like crying . . . (*continues to cry*).

61 *Anne:* I'd feel better for having that baby 'cos I know, that if I had another handicapped child that she'd be able to cope with it . . . I mean when the baby's like that and they sat up all night. She was home and everything. They really loved her . . .

62 *Mandy:* Oh no . . . me eyes are running . . .

63 *Sue:* Oh no . . .

64 *Anne:* . . . she was a gorgeous baby.

At the end of this dialogue, Mandy and Sue were moved to tears. This is a personal and deeply-felt learning experience which could not have happened other than amongst a group of friends in a 'private' situation dealing with a subject important to them in an open and honest way. Can you imagine such a response to a set of closed comprehension questions on a passage about handicapped children? During this tape the girls are using talk to explore their feelings and reactions to imagined situations.

They have moved from the 'shallow end' of known, stock response to a deeper area where their feelings and attitudes are unknown, yet to be discovered. The webs of thought and feeling are revealed at first by open questions: 'Do you think you'd be able to cope?' (4). No easy answers here. Anne is groping for her answer when in response to Jane's 'I wouldn't disown it' (25), she says 'I would ... I don't think ... I think it all depends' (26).

Jane wisely says: 'You've got to be in the situation first' (20). In a way, this is what the girls are doing here. They are thinking and feeling their way into an unknown situation, thereby reaching an understanding of the dilemma faced by others and coming to terms with their own feelings and responses. I want to make grand claims for what the girls are doing here. To my mind this is education at its best and purest. They are, together, leading each other on towards a closer understanding of self and others. Empathy and self-awareness mingle and grow. The contributions to the conversation become almost as one as they explore the issue that enmeshes them. It is a supportive, collaborative discussion in the most fruitful sense. Here is no polarity. Complicated feelings are mapped and expressed. The contours of the mind are revealed.

Yet it was not too morbid or sombre a discussion. In (27) Mandy comments on Jane's wriggling about on the uncomfortable chairs: 'Have you got bum ache?' Jane cuffs her and is in turn disciplined by Mandy: 'Don't be silly' (36). Had teacher spotted this he might well have intervened and broken up the discussion. In that way the most important moments may well have been lost. The girls are as capable of achieving self-discipline here as they are of self-knowledge.

I have tried in the book so far to offer some points about the philosophical context of using talk-for-learning and to illustrate and give life to those ideas by examples of talk-for-learning at work. What do these examples have in common? What are the essential features of fruitful talk-for-learning?

Firstly, in all the examples quoted the children are operating at the sharp end of thought and feeling. They are exploring, making sense of new ideas and experiences. They are developing new understanding of the world around them and by implication of themselves and others. In Nigel and Annette's cases, talking opens out their potential for new language, new thoughts, and for the shaping of an experience in the imagination to create coherent meaning. The 12-year-old 'scientists', whilst co-operating on a common, purposeful task, are through talk, developing their powers of scientific thinking: logic, speculation, hypothesising and problem-solving. Again they are operating at the frontier of their intellectual capability, a frontier marked by their tentativeness, their willingness to be wrong. The girls in the last extract are working in the same kind of way but with the exploration of feeling at the centre. All, in a way, are sorting through thoughts and feelings in an attempt to make sense of themselves and the world, to fit new bits into the jigsaws in their heads, to enable the picture of the world to emerge from the developing tray.

I believe that for most children this kind of development is best achieved through talk. Writing is a very middle-class and laborious activity. I have seen some very impressive learning-logs written by teachers and some written by more able children. Medway (1984) points out that the feature shared by the kind of talk and writing useful for learning (in the sense of shaping meaning) was that it was expressive. I shall deal later with the threat that expressive modes would appear to pose to the teaching and learning models teachers have, and have no wish to set up a dichotomy between talk and writing. They can both be powerful means to learn.

But for the vast majority of children for whom writing is a struggle (and I refer both to younger children and all but the more able older pupils) talk is the most natural and flexible medium to catch thought on the wing and thereby to journey around the so-far-unknown areas of the mind.

5 Patterns of talk in schools

Who needs the most practice talking in school? Who gets the most? Exactly: the children need it, the teacher gets it.

William Hull

The thinking of educationalists, over at least the last 20 years, about the central role that talk plays in successful learning can be illustrated by examples of such talk in action such as I have quoted in the last chapter. How much of this thinking has filtered through to schools in the last two decades? How typical are the examples given above of the daily experience in schools? How much 'learning-talk' happens in everyday classrooms and does it therefore have the central role in practice that the theory claims it should have?

It is very difficult to give authoritative answers to these questions simply because the necessary research has yet to be done and would be very difficult indeed to undertake. Many researchers (for example, Flanders 1962) have observed and quantified classroom activity, but as yet no one has done so based on the kind of definition of 'learning-talk' offered in this book. We have evidence of how much *talk* goes on in classrooms, but as yet little analysis of the quality and nature of these exchanges.

It would be accepted, however, by all concerned, that learning-talk does not have a central importance in British classrooms. This belief would be based both on the gut reaction of experience and on concern expressed about the neglect of talk in recent official surveys. In this chapter I will begin by examining briefly the evidence offered in those official reports and continue by describing some small-scale enquiries of my own which may shed some light on the situation.

The Bullock Report (DES 1975) collected much of its factual evidence on what was happening in the classroom in a way which is not quite broad or reliable enough for us to draw convincing conclusions about the amount of learning-talk happening in schools in the early 1970s. First, it concentrated in the secondary sector on what was happening in *English* departments, which does not give us a picture of talk in the whole school experience. Second, it relied on what teachers said (or thought) they were doing rather than on the evidence of actual classroom observation.

Nevertheless, it does present data which may give us some pointers about the pattern of talk. Table 1 is a summary of the Bullock Report evidence on the time spent on oral English by six- and nine-year-olds.

What can we learn from this? Whatever conclusions are drawn must be at best tentative. What did the teachers mean by 'oral English'? Did they refer only to those activities labelled in their minds as 'English'? Would a group discussion of a piece of scientific work be included in their time schedules? As the authors of the report mention in their analysis, 'Since oral work pervades almost the whole of the work in the primary school, it must be acknowledged that a question asking how much time was spent on it in a week has an element of artificiality' (p. 390). Nevertheless, within their definition of 'conversation, language games, planning work, discussion, reporting' (and excluding drama), the authors report that '41 per cent of 6 year olds and 56 per cent of 9 year olds spent no optional time at all on oral work'. Furthermore, 'only 66 per cent of the 9 year olds spent more than half an hour a week of both class *and* optional time on it' (compared with 86 per cent of six-year-olds). The authors conclude: 'The distribution of higher time allocations shows that the amount of explicit attention to oral English declines substantially from 6 years old to 9 years old' (p. 390).

The evidence from the report would seem to indicate that the decline continues in the secondary sector. Here one must assume they gathered their evidence from the many experienced witnesses called rather than from statistics. I would suggest that this evidence, though subjective, is quite possibly more reliable than that based on their survey of teachers' perceptions of an inadequately defined area. The authors conclude:

> In many of [the pupils'] specialist subject lessons in the secondary school, the experience is likely to give him much less scope for exploratory talk [than in the primary school]. There is a greater probability of direct teaching, with the teacher controlling the lesson by question and answer, and the pupils' responses shepherded within defined limits (p. 141).

Later there is a more explicit judgement dealing with language across the curriculum:

> When we consider the working day in a secondary school the neglect of pupil talk as a valuable means of learning stands out sharply.... Where pupil talk has been accorded little status in teaching methods, it is not surprising that when the opportunity does occur it tends to be filled by pointless chatter (p. 189).

A telling piece of evidence is cited:

>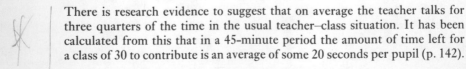
> There is research evidence to suggest that on average the teacher talks for three quarters of the time in the usual teacher–class situation. It has been calculated from this that in a 45-minute period the amount of time left for a class of 30 to contribute is an average of some 20 seconds per pupil (p. 142).

Table 1. Time spent on oral English (conversation, language games, planning work, discussion, reporting) by six- and nine-year-olds.

	Classes spending these amounts of class time (*minutes*)							All classes	
	0	1–30	31–60	61–90	91–120	121–150	151 or more	No.	(%)
Six-year-olds									
Optional time (minutes)									
0	11	105	152	140	80	46	46	580	*40·9*
1–30	6	83	140	102	56	27	26	440	*31·1*
31–60	6	11	53	52	27	25	13	187	*13·2*
61–90	3	4	11	30	14	13	16	91	*6·4*
91–120		3	3	6	12	3	1	28	*2·0*
121–150	1	1	2	6	3	4	5	22	*1·6*
151 or more		6	10	5	8	6	34	69	*4·9*
All classes	27	213	371	341	200	124	141	1,417	
As a percentage of all classes	*1·9*	*15·0*	*26·2*	*24·1*	*14·1*	*8·8*	*10·0*		*100·0*
Nine-year-olds									
Optional time (minutes)									
0	42	249	238	104	46	15	12	706	*56·3*
1–30	28	105	123	70	17	7	9	359	*28·7*
31–60	8	20	39	37	17		3	124	*9·9*
61–90	2	4	11	9	4	5		35	*2·8*
91–120	2		2	4	5	2	2	17	*1·4*
121 150		1			4			5	*0·4*
151 or more	1			1			5	7	*0·6*
All classes	83	379	413	225	93	29	31	1,253	
As a percentage of all classes	*6·6*	*30·3*	*33·0*	*18·0*	*7·4*	*2·3*	*2·5*		*100·0*

Source: DES (1975, p. 390).

Presumably the research ties in with that of Flanders (1962) quoted by Harold Rosen in Barnes *et al.* (1969, p. 120): 'In the average classroom, someone is talking for two-thirds of the time, two-thirds of the talk is teacher-talk, and two-thirds of the teacher talk is direct influence'. I can only confirm that in my experience schools have not changed radically enough since that era to make such an analysis seem now either dated or preposterous.

Four years after Bullock came the HMI survey *Primary Education in England* (DES 1978). Had the wise thoughts of the Bullock Committee had any impact on primary schools in such a short time? The 1978 survey is a disappointingly bland and dry document lacking the fire, vigour and persuasive articulacy of the Bullock Report.

It contains a rather bare and lifeless section on talk (pp. 46–7) with, it appears, a model of talk in mind which is depressingly passive. The authors remark cheerfully on the finding that children seemed to be listening to their teachers more and to greater effect: 'In over nine out of ten classes children were learning to follow instructions effectively, to understand the main ideas in information given to them and to follow the plot of a story.'

Yet a warning note begins to sound in the next paragraph:

> Although four-fifths of year old classes were learning to comprehend the details in information they were given, in only about three-fifths of these classes were children learning to follow a sustained discussion and contribute appropriately and in fewer still were the children taught to follow the line of an argument.

The Inspectors then go on to report optimistically that 'In almost all the classes children had the opportunity to talk informally amongst themselves at some time in the course of the working day'. One would certainly hope so! The alternative of a silent school is surely one which not even the staunchest contributor to the *Black Papers* could advocate. As the children grow older, the Inspectors notice an increase in the opportunity for more formal arrangements for conversation which allowed controlled exchanges of ideas between children. In two-thirds of seven-year-old classes and almost half the nine and 11-year-old classes children were given 'the opportunity to discuss with their teachers the work they are doing and the problems they meet'. Again a surprisingly bland and complacent statement. Can we tolerate so calmly a situation whereby in over half of the classes of nine- and 11-year-olds, the children are not being given a chance to discuss their work with their teachers?

The report goes on to comment that in nine-tenths of classes the children's vocabulary was 'steadily extended', in half the classes children were 'encouraged to elaborate and explain their answers or comments' and in only about a fifth of the classes were the children encouraged to ask questions, 'or helped to find alternative ways of expressing themselves clearly and accurately'.

I suspect that the answers provided by the 1978 survey are not useful to us in judging how much fruitful learning-talk is going on in schools, because I do not think the Inspectors had a clear idea of what they were looking for, and hence ended up asking the wrong questions. There is no mention of purposeful discussion in small groups, or of the kind of tentative, collaborative and expressive talk which is so central to the development of language and understanding. Rather, I feel that HMI established in this survey that there was a lot of passive-talk activity going on. Perhaps the messages of Bullock had got through but only in a distorted version.

The next major survey of this era, *Aspects of Secondary Education in England* (DES 1979), is much more helpful to us in assessing how much 'learning-talk' exists in schools. The Inspectors responsible for this document would appear to share the enlightened view of talk established in the Bullock Report. Besides being a better-written report, it is much clearer in its assumptions about good and bad learning models. It wastes little time getting to the heart of the problem of talk in schools:

> Although considerable research over the last 20 years into the ways in which language is acquired and extended has emphasised the part that talking can play in learning, the evidence of the survey indicated that this is still not widely known among teachers. Pupils usually spent more time in reading and writing than they did in talking and listening; and in the oral exchanges between class and teacher very much more time listening than talking (p. 94).

My own observations above very much echo this view and the picture presented here is a very familiar one: 'There were many examples of lengthy monologues without pause for questions, often accompanied by dutiful note-making by pupils' (p. 95). Typical of the restrained yet enlightened approach of the Inspectors in this document, they add with touching understatement: 'Pupils who spend so much of their time listening may need more opportunities than they are given to confirm their understanding and to relate it to other experience'. However they do note in this report 'a diversity of practice' and, without any attempts to quantify, mention that there were in existence 'schools where teachers had recognised that talk was a means by which pupils could take an active part in learning ... and encouraged pupils to initiate discussion, to speculate and to offer differing views'. Nevertheless I get the impression throughout this report that such teachers and such schools were the exception, who for some reason or other had 'seen the light' and that the old practices stubbornly carried on as before in most other schools.

Seven years after the Bullock Report, HMI published a short follow-up document called *Bullock Revisited* (DES 1982). It is interesting to us in the context of this chapter as it could give a clear indication of whether the urgent concerns articulated in 1974 had been attended to in schools since that date. Marginal progress is reported in paragraph 3.5, p. 5, referring to the three major surveys so far mentioned here: 'Since these reports were published many Primary and Secondary schools have given greater opportunities for pupils to engage in discussion and to express their ideas in speech'. Progress perhaps. But a more fundamental issue is raised by the next comment: 'Nevertheless, in many schools, aims, objectives and methods for promoting oral language need to be more clearly defined'. Hinted at here is a concern which I share and which is explored more fully in the next section of this book: namely that teachers are not clear enough about the kinds of talk they should be promoting in schools and, by implication, they are unsure about exactly how to promote it.

During 1984 definitive results emerged from Gordon Wells's study of the language development of children in Bristol, though some tempting titbits had been offered since the early finding of the late 1970s. A number of his observations are of interest to us in considering patterns of learning talk in schools. In Wells and Wells (1984) he first acknowledges 'that there is often a gap between theory and practice' in the matter of the use of talk in schools, and goes on to refer to a research study by Wood *et al.* (1980) which found that practitioners in nursery schools and playgroups were surprised to discover how little extended conversation actually went on in their classrooms. This finding was, incidentally, echoed by a small-scale piece of research I conducted amongst 50 fourth- and fifth-years in 1986 which revealed that a third of the sample had not the opportunity for extended discussion with tutors or subject teachers during a particular school year and only a sixth reported having a regular opportunity. Observations of the students in lessons confirmed this in its finding that only 13 per cent of teacher–pupil contacts were 'extended', in that they lasted for longer than three minutes. Seventy per cent took less than 30 seconds.

Wells's work in Bristol makes a fascinating comparison between opportunities for fruitful 'learning-talk' at home and at the infant stage at school. In Wells and Wells (1984) he concludes that,

> compared with their experiences at home, children at school were found to play a much less active role in conversation. They initiated fewer exchanges, asked fewer questions and took fewer turns per interaction. Their utterances were syntactically simpler, contained a narrower range of semantic content and less frequently referred outside the here and now.

Wells comments on the familiar pattern of talk in schools when he concludes

> In contrast with their parents, the children's teachers dominated conversation, initiating the majority of interactions, predominantly through questions and requests. They were also more than twice as likely to develop their own meanings as they were to extend those contributed by the children.

His most startling revelation is that 'There were *no* homes that did not provide richer opportunities than the schools for learning through talk with an adult'.

The final publication I shall refer to here was produced under the auspices of Sir Keith Joseph in 1985. In *Better Schools* (DES 1985a) one must imagine that he drew heavily on the independent evidence provided by HMI. There are clear hints in this that schools have still not taken on board wholeheartedly the messages from successive major reports and, more importantly, from the thinking of educationalists which provide the philosophical foundation for those reports. There are complaints in Chapter 1 Section 18 about the 'mistaken belief . . . [that] concentration on basic skills is by itself enough to improve achievement in literacy'. The report claims that 'in a majority of schools' there is an 'overconcentration on the practice of basic skills . . . unrelated to a context in which they are needed'. Though talk is not specifically mentioned here, the implication for the purposes of this book is that the kind of talk for learning earlier described has not taken on a powerful and prominent role, ten years after Bullock.

At best, then, the major DES reports and other related research commenting on the quality and kind of learning provided in schools present a consistent picture to us: talk for learning still does not play a key part in the education of young people in schools.

If the evidence above gives the broad, 'official' sweep of evidence, I would like now to shed some light on those findings with some smaller-scale enquiries of my own conducted since 1980. During 1981 I undertook an investigation into the changing nature of the learning experience at the primary–secondary changeover point. My particular focus was on the language demands made on pupils. During this investigation I spent a day with each of three pupils during their last term at the primary school (in two different schools and three different classrooms) and followed this up by spending a day with them six weeks into their first term at the nearby secondary school. Whilst working alongside the pupils I noted exactly what activities they were involved in and the demands made of them. This was quite difficult to do and inevitably involved some rationalisation. I had forgotten that you can write, talk to your friend and kick the child opposite you at the same time. Nevertheless, the statistics presented in Table 2 give us an interesting overview of how time was spent during these six days.

Let me clarify the points which are less than obvious. The disparity between 'available teaching time' and time when the pupil is 'actively engaged in lessons' is caused by my subtracting time spent idling and waiting, changing, moving and settling. At times my judgements were inevitably subjective. What about when the pupil is staring into space during a Maths test, thinking, having a breather or daydreaming? 'Listening to the teacher talk' refers to straight lectures or explanations, not the kind which is interspersed with questions or brief discussion, which I've called

Table 2. Time analysis of three pupils' school days at primary and secondary school.

Activity	Samantha		Andrew		Michael	
	Primary hrs mins	Secondary hrs mins	Primary hrs mins	Secondary hrs mins	Primary hrs mins	Secondary hrs mins
General breakdown of the school day						
Available teaching time	4·20	4·55	4·37	4·55	4·40	5·05
Breaks/lunchtimes	1·45	1·30	1·45	1·30	1·30	1·30
Assembly and admin. time	0·20	0·30	0·03	0·30	0·00	0·20
Overall school day	6·25	6·55	6·25	6·55	6·10	6·55
Available teaching time						
Actively engaged in lessons	3·38	3·56	3·07	4·06	3·53	3·49
Waiting/changing/ moving/settling down/ clearing up	0·40	0·50	0·50	0·37	0·30	0·59
Idling	0·02	0·09	0·40	0·12	0·17	0·17
Total	4·20	4·55	4·37	4·55	4·40	5·05
Talking/listening						
Listening to teacher talk	0·25	0·50	0·11	0·39	0·12	0·33
Individual discussion with teacher	0·10	0·05	0·02	0·01	0·09	0·05
'Closed' class discussion	0·00	0·39	0·00	0·35	0·00	0·33
'Open' class discussion	0·02	0·05	0·00	0·33	0·00	0·18
Small group/pair talk	0·08	0·00	0·05	0·00	0·04	0·00
Drama	0·00	0·00	0·00	0·00	0·00	0·00
Listening/responding to tape	0·00	0·00	0·00	0·08	0·00	0·00
Total	0·45	1·39	0·18	1·56	0·25	1·29
Writing						
Copying	0·05	0·09	0·00	0·14	0·10	0·14
'Free' writing	0·45	0·00	0·40	0·00	0·06	0·00
Note-making	0·00	0·00	0·00	0·00	0·00	0·00
Factual	0·00	0·00	0·00	0·00	0·00	0·16
Answers to questions	0·00	0·10	0·00	0·00 -	0·11	0·13
To think/speculate	0·00	0·00	0·00	0·00	0·00	0·11
Total	0·50	0·19	0·40	0·14	0·27	0·54
Reading						
Privately for pleasure	0·05	0·00	0·05	0·00	0·18	0·00
Aloud	0·02	0·00	0·00	0·00	0·01	0·00
Listening to	0·14	0·31	0·02	0·41	0·10	0·00
For purpose/information	0·00	0·00	0·00	0·13	0·13	0·00
Total	0·21	0·31	0·07	0·54	0·42	0·00
Other activities						
PE/games	0·25	0·00	0·00	0·00	1·01	0·23
Practical – experimental	0·00	0·00	0·00	0·00	0·22	0·00
Practical – creative	0·00	0·43	1·14	0·46	0·53	0·41
Maths sums/problems	0·47	0·44	0·40	0·14	0·03	0·22
Various other	0·30	–	0·08	–	–	–

Activity	Samantha		Andrew		Michael	
	Primary hrs mins	Secondary hrs mins	Primary hrs mins	Secondary hrs mins	Primary hrs mins	Secondary hrs mins
Questions from the teacher						
'Open'	?	3	?	2	?	3
'Closed'	?	111	?	72	?	81
Questions from the child						
To teacher	?	11	?	1	?	2
To peers	?	7	?	2	?	1

'closed class discussion'. In an 'open class discussion' the class was invited to participate in a relatively wide-ranging discussion with little or no 'right answer', where the children could contribute their views and experiences freely. My three pupils did not always contribute to the class discussions, but during the times on the chart they were at least participating by listening attentively. Small group or pair talk does not refer to what I classed in a biased and arbitrary way as 'unrelated gossip' (which went down under 'idling'). These were not silent classrooms. I noticed that the pupils I observed could also gossip and chatter away whilst doing certain kinds of activity – for example, copying or drawing. Later in this chapter I will present an analysis of what I see as the educational value of the talk that takes place in this way.

The section on questions was added during the secondary pupils' days when the need suddenly arose. They do not necessarily refer to *personal* questions. Ninety per cent of them were questions thrown out to the class as a whole, which my three pupils could have answered had they wished to do so (and did sometimes). I have no recollections of questions being asked in the primary school, largely because that particular teaching style was not in evidence. Had I recorded questions on the primary days I am certain that no category would have reached double figures.

I classed an 'open' question as one which at least invited a variety of possible answers, at best invited a completely individual response (for example, 'Would anyone tell me about a time that you have been scared?'). Some questions masqueraded as open questions, but the teachers' responses to the answers showed that they were in effect 'closed' questions; remember the albatross?

This evidence raises a number of issues. First the time spent on talk/listening activities generally is disappointingly small and does not correspond with the observations by Flanders (1962), quoted above. From a total of 22 hours 29 minutes spent 'actively engaged in lessons' during the six days, only 6 hours 32 minutes were spent on talk-type activities. This represents 29 per cent of learning activity, compared with the 75 per cent quoted in the Bullock Report and the 66 per cent assessment by Flanders.

Though the three sets of figures emerge from differing standpoints, if my analysis is in any way representative or reliable, one could get depressed.

In the breakdown of my pupils' days, if we subtract the time spent listening to the teacher talk in a 'lecture' format, we are left with a mere 16 per cent of classroom activity spent on more educational kinds of talk. Furthermore very little of that time was spent in small group or pair work which this book will argue provides the most fruitful context for learning-talk. Only 18 minutes was spent in this way in the whole of the three primary school days; in the secondary phase this had dwindled to nothing.

Schools and classrooms, we all know, are full of talk. But it would appear to be the wrong *kind* of talk. It is as if the message put across during the last 20 years about the value of talk has been heard by teachers, but only partially; like a Chinese whisper it has been distorted and changed since the original message was passed on by the authors of the Bullock Report. Accepting the Flanders 'two-thirds' observation, I would go on to say that the talk I observe in schools as taking up the lion's share of this reported 66 per cent of classroom activity falls into two categories:

1 Teachers engaging in closed whole-class discussion.
2 Pupils chattering 'off task' while they work.

Let me reflect a while on the nature and value of these two kinds of talk from the learner's point of view.

Silting up the channels

In Barnes *et al.* (1969) Barnes offered a telling exposé of what I have called 'closed class discussion'. He does this in terms of the interaction of the learner, the teacher and the subject – it is essentially a sociolinguistic approach. Since this kind of discussion still appears to me to be the staple diet of many secondary school classrooms it is worth looking at an example 17 years after the ones Barnes presents, in the light of more recent thinking about language and learning.

This short extract is from a team-taught lesson with 13-year-old pupils in a mixed-ability Humanities class in 1986. The topic is natural disasters and the class is focusing its attention on flooding. They have some textbooks in front of them and there has been some discussion about pictures.

> *Teacher:* Of course as rivers flow down towards the sea they carry with them large quantities of what? Not just water, but large quantities of ...?
> *Boy A:* Stuff and rubbish?
> *Teacher:* That's right ... well, yes, what do you mean by ... stuff and

rubbish is a bit imprecise as a term ... I mean you're talking about old tin cans and bits of trees and things, aren't you? Well it's a bit more than that. What does it carry? ... Rod?

Rod: Sewage?

Teacher: Well, it might carry sewage ... Yes ... it might ...

Boy B: Houses?

Teacher: Houses ... well I'm not thinking necessarily of when it goes into flood ... Sadie?

Sadie: Debris?

Teacher: Debris ... possibly ... David?

David: Silt?

Teacher: That's right, silt.

What is happening here? Presumably the teacher has a concept in mind that he wants the pupils to understand: that quantities of silt are carried downstream by a river and are eventually deposited at the point it joins the sea. So we have if you like a content-based learning model. There are things that the teacher knows that the pupils need to know. The chosen method of getting that content across is to have a whole-class closed discussion. By that I mean that the teacher wants to talk about it to the class and include them by asking a sprinkling of closed questions. Presumably this form is chosen rather than a straight lecture as it keeps the majority of children alert, tests understanding as the teacher goes along and acts as a kind of public revelation of 'the true facts'. This may or may not be more effective than a straight, well-prepared and illustrated lecturette. I strongly suspect that the pupils see this kind of activity as a sort of game which they largely avoid being involved in, and do their best to please the teacher when asked. In this situation it is not surprising that the pupils contribute very little: just seven words compared to the teacher's 98.

There is evidence here that, in terms of the learning of content, things are not going well. First, there seems to be a fundamental misunderstanding about the context of the teacher's questions. The class, carried on by the momentum of the earlier discussion about flooding, still have the picture of the flood in their mind. So the 'stuff and rubbish' and the 'sewage' refer to things carried down by the river at a time of a serious flood. The answer 'Houses?' confirms this ... the teacher reveals in response that he suspects this misunderstanding but proceeds with the same line of questioning. It is evident that he is after one word here: 'silt'. Other contributions are handled gently, with some encouragement. No one is put down or made to feel ignorant; there are no straight denials; all answers are *possible*, but it's evidently silt or nothing. There are tensions and pressures emerging in this approach. The pupils are all past experts at recognising the rules of this particular game of 'guess what's in the teacher's head'. They become more tentative and less confident in the answers they offer (and in a sense more off-beam in their responses). The atmosphere stiffens during the discussion and the teacher has to work harder to elicit responses. The pupils are gambling; the risk is the exposure of public ignorance, the rewards the seal of approval for the 'right' answer. Yet I must emphasise that this is not a repressive or a 'traditional' classroom. Indeed the teacher had an easy and relaxed rapport with the pupils. Later in this book I shall analyse closely a sequence of work leading from this initial whole-class discussion which contains some excellent examples of learning-talk. This is an enlightened, humane and well-liked teacher at work.

Why does this particular sequence come out quite as it does, then? I have already mentioned the content-based learning model, but perhaps more fundamental than that is the teacher's image of himself. Teachers, by nature of their title, calling and the received traditions of our culture, have a role engrained on them as dispensers of knowledge rather than as providers of opportunities. Teachers, it seems, need to feel active, in control, leading the relatively passive learners hither and thither, rather like well-versed couriers on a coach tour. Such a position is perhaps addictively attractive to many of us. Knowing the right answer puts us in a position of some power, which gives in a sense the same kind of boost to our egos as telling a good joke, or tantalising groups of people with those De Bono lateral thinking problems. In recent years teachers have felt increasingly under threat and it is no wonder that they cling desperately and instinctively to the powerful vestiges of a discredited methodology. I am not here wishing to write off all whole-class discussion as valueless. Examples will be presented later of teachers leading much more helpful and fruitful class discussion. Suffice to assert that closed-class discussion of this kind is still widespread in secondary classrooms and is largely ineffective in its presumed aims of putting content across to pupils: it also discourages pupils from becoming involved in the more fundamental processes of learning. If teachers were more aware of the dangerously anti-educational forces at work during this kind of very common set of exchanges they would wish to wean themselves off them.

In place of silence: on-task chatter revealed

I am aware that in my pupil-day analysis I was rather dismissive of pupil 'gossip' or the chatter they engage in whilst undertaking other 'non-talk' tasks. During my action-research year in a family of schools a teacher asked me whether I knew what children talk about when they are working. She was concerned to run an open classroom where pupils worked in groups round clusters of desks and where talking was seen as part of the learning process. She was aware that there was a lot of talk all the time when the children were at work, but was not sure whether it was 'on-task' talk, whether it was unrelated gossip (in which case, was it educational in the wider sense?) or whether it distracted from or enhanced the task in hand. These were questions with wide implications and which inevitably begged a number of more fundamental questions (such as what is learning?), but I was aware that a fascinating area for investigation was opening up in front of me which could also shed light on some of the assumptions of my earlier enquiry. Children had talked a lot in my classrooms too, but whenever I had tried to 'tap into' it, it seemed that my presence, or the presence of a tape recorder, radically changed what had happened. What was the nature of everyday classroom chatter? Did it differ in any fundamental way from common-or-garden playground talk? (And what value does *that* have?)

It was evident that I would not be able to begin to answer these questions unless I could somehow sit in on a number of examples of classroom chatter. It was no good my assuming a teacherly role: I had to become a pupil for a while. Accordingly I was introduced to a Humanities class as someone who was interested in joining in the work of the class to see what it was like and I spent several sessions simply working alongside groups of children, doing the tasks that they were doing. It did not take long, it seemed, for me to be accepted as a fixture. Early on, I felt instinctively that my presence had in fact affected the agenda for discussion, but soon it appeared that I was completely ignored; the activity and talk around me flowed on as normal. By just listening and making the odd note I was able to gain some important insights. Before long I was able to take a portable tape recorder along with me, at first simply leaving it lying around to get people used to it, and then towards the end of the project, switching it on from time to time. I did this with their permission, but without their feeling they were the focus of attention, for I had said I was simply interested in the general level of classroom noise. In this way I was able to monitor about eight hours of classroom chatter and have tape recordings of over three hours of it. Your judgement on this evidence is very much tied up with your view of what learning is. To be, in my terms, 'learning talk', it would need to have some developmental element in it – that is, the learner should be journeying towards some understanding of the self, of others or of the world around him or her. I am expecting and looking for small steps only, but the learner must surely be groping forward in some significant way.

Here is a typical example of the talk I encountered. Three boys are working separately on a report on our planet by an alien visitor. The idea has enormous potential. One boy had weaved into this a picture of Bulldog Bobby which he was lovingly drawing and colouring.

Graham: This does not look like a pair of shorts because it isn't a pair of shorts.
Lennie: Are you doing that one of Bulldog Bobby?
Graham: Mmm ... I'll have a go ... I've got him all on my bedspread.
Lennie: Have you?
Graham: Yes.

Lennie: All over?
Graham: Yes ... and Bryan Robson, Gary Lineker and Peter Shilton ... I don't like any of them.
Lennie: All over your bedspread?
Graham: Yes ... it's an England bedspread.
Lennie: I guessed that.
Graham: What?
Lennie: I guessed that.
Graham: Mmm ... I wanted a Scotland one.
Lennie: Huh! Do you support Scotland?
Graham: No ... because the Scotland one had Kenny Dalglish on it.
Lennie: Do you like Kenny Dalglish and all?
Graham: He's my favourite player.
Lennie: Manager/player.
Graham: I didn't like him as a manager, I liked him as a player ... good player ... Right. This is a bit ... I can't draw the legs ... so this will look dead funny ... ooh! ... I got it right for once ... that really looks like a leg ... with a bandage on.
         (*Lennie then reads out a piece of his writing, half to himself, half aloud.*)
Graham: There ... what a jazzy football boot.

One thing is clear: they are not talking about the topic that the teacher would see as the central concern of the lesson. I also find it very difficult indeed to find any educational value whatsoever in this talk. There's a kind of Pete-and-Dud humour in it at times (particularly in the talk about the bedspread) but it is not a humour that the boys relish or are even aware of. The whole exchange is amusing because of its unbearably trivial content. One cannot help congratulating the third boy from keeping well out of it. In many ways this is not a conversation at all, in that there is little evidence, if any, of a meeting of minds. Looked at in this way, Graham's utterances are best seen as a kind of necessary self-expression, a personalised running commentary on what he is doing, made acceptable by the fact that there is an audience present but in reality directed inwards, in a self-maintaining capacity. They simply replace the silence, fill the social vacuum around him and hence create (perhaps) a more pleasant working environment. I have hours of such chatter on tape. It is like a kind of classroom wallpaper, relieving the blank spaces.

Here is a similar example from a table full of girls, on the same (separate but similar) task.

Chris: Sue, where's that ruler?
Sue: Kathy ... Tipp-Ex, please.
Chris: Where's that ruler I lent you, Sue? I've got stomach-ache chewing ... (*indistinct*) ... they're gorgeous ... They've got an awful flavour but ... I'll take it out ... I'll take it out, right ... In a couple of minutes ... ooo!

Sue: Let's see who can keep it out the longest
Chris: Right ... go.
          (*Three seconds' pause*)
Chris: You!! (*Laughter*)
Kathy: You'll get done for eating that you know.
Chris: I won't, Miss Larkin's seen me.
Kathy: You'll still get done ... if Mr Davies sees you, you're for it.
Chris: Whoops-a-daisy ...
Sue: Mr Davies ain't down here.

There is a desire to communicate here which needs to be channelled into something purposeful. Though indicative of a nice, well-adjusted set of social relations, the discussion here is merely a rehearsal of emptiness, but one which I suspect only needs the right context, the right spark, to bring learning back to life.

Did the pupils *never* talk about the task in hand? I did find the odd moment when the set work of the classroom flickered across their consciousnesses. In this example the boys are completing (separately) a worksheet on a medieval village, which included a picture of a wattle-and-daub house.

Dave: They look like quite good houses, don't they?
Ian: They're alright ... fairly big.
Stuart: That's wattle and daub, innit?
Dave: Bet it took a lot of time making, though.
Stuart: Yeah.
Dave: You seen them doing it today. [There is a new, executive housing estate under construction in the area.] They're original stone, original beams. They cost a bomb.
Ian: Yeah!
Stuart: Barry Drive ... That's in Kirby, innit?
Dave: What?
Ian: That's where Edmonds lives, innit?
Dave: What?
Ian: Barry Drive.
Stuart: Is that the rich part?
Dave: No idea (*indistinct*) Barry Drive's got £80,000 houses on it.
Ian: Flippin' eck.
          (*Twenty seconds' pause*)
Ian: Leicester Forest East.
Stuart: It's rich up there, innit?
Ian: Yes, near LFE, some of the places ... because they've got that massive hotel there, haven't they?
Dave: Yeah, because I know of that hotel because we always take a short cut through.
Ian: Everybody says you shouldn't go down there, but we used to go right through. Takes about an extra 15 miles. I mean you can cut straight through there ... you'd save about ten miles.

Perhaps we can value this more highly than the other examples. Early on there is an attempt to evaluate medieval houses and to think their way into the effort of building them. We can perhaps be pleased at the way they relate that with their own experience of houses being built – but from this promising start the conversation lapses into a mode as trivial as the other two examples: a filling of the threatening empty spaces of silence with a bit of light-hearted commentary and banter.

I am aware that there are educationalists who might be tempted to construct their castles of meaning on the three examples I have quoted. All sorts of justifications could be offered which one is tempted to parody. I firmly believe that the rationalisation of what is essentially an over-whelmingly trivial set of exchanges does the gravest possible disservice to the development of fruitful learning-talk in our schools. This is the unacceptable face of oracy. If teachers are led to mistake such classroom chance encounters for the genuine meeting of minds that can be created by committed and purposeful dialogue, the school experience will be the poorer for it. Bullock makes an oblique reference to the problem and supports my value judgement (DES 1975, p. 189): 'Where pupil talk has been accorded little status in teaching methods, it is not surprising that when the opportunity does occur it tends to be filled by pointless chatter'. Richmond (1983) states the point rather more clearly and baldly: 'There's a big difference between disruptive chatter and constructive talking to learn'.

In many ways the pupils would be better served if told to work in silence. It was clearly evident that the talk, though relieving the pressure of silence, distracted the pupils from any task that involved a cognitive act. Copying, drawing, decorating title-pages could all sustain being overlaid with such chatter without being interrupted. But whenever the pupils were having to process or interpret some materials through their brain – in other words, whenever they were required to take on an active, thinking role – the chatter inevitably replaced the cognitive tasks and became a less demanding, more relaxed alternative to it.

I would not wish to denigrate all informal exchanges between young people as existing on this trivial level. We may be tempted to imagine that all communication amongst them is reflected by this bored gossip during lesson time. How often do we teachers refer rather snootily to 'corridor talk' or 'playground talk' as if it were something on a lower level than the heightened exchanges of the classroom. The small-scale enquiry referred to earlier, conducted amongst 50 14- and 15-year-olds in 1986 suggests that the opposite may be true. In contrast to their lack of opportunity for extended talk with the adult teachers and tutors they encountered, those teenagers reported the existence of a very strong peer-group forum for intense and personal talk which provided them with the support network apparently denied them by the school. Seventy-seven per cent of them claimed to have had regular discussions of this nature with peers during the current school year. In follow-up interviews the students were probed about this but were insistent about the amount of serious talking-through of issues that goes on amongst them during 'unofficial' time both in and out of school. As one girl said: 'You can have a good laugh with your mates, but if I've got anything on my mind I always go to my mates first; they're the only ones that listen'. Pupils in the school I am currently working in say that they have had serious discussions about AIDS with their friends but not so far with teachers and parents. How ironic that being in lessons would appear to squeeze out from them this capacity for sustained and serious discussion. I can only conclude that the trivial 'wallpaper' talk I encountered is merely a refuge from the boredom of the lesson, a counter to the enervating process of ploughing through the given curriculum.

So it is my clear impression that the two-thirds share that talk has of classroom activity is largely taken up by the teacher-dominated closed-class discussion, and by the kind of on-task chatter described above. If that is the case, then learning-talk has an even smaller place in schools than the earlier-quoted official reports suggest. I would go so far as to say that such talk is rare enough, certainly in secondary schools, for us to conclude that the consensus of the last 20 years of educational thought about language and learning in schools has not impinged to any significant extent on the everyday classroom experience of young people.

We owe someone an explanation.

6 Bricks in the wall

> The great mistake we educationalists make is to suppose that schools are about education ... schools are about control.
> R. F. Mackenzie

> All teachers use talk for controlling and organizing children and as an essential aid in teaching; talk is used to inform and instruct, to expound ideas, to question and check on children's learning, to evaluate children's work and behaviour and for many other purposes. In all schools children are expected to be alert to the meaning of teachers' talk, to interpret and respond appropriately; talk plays an important part in schools in communicating to children what teachers expect of them. But what place do teachers give to children's talk? Children are frequently expected to answer teachers' questions, and may be encouraged to ask questions and take part in discussion. But many teachers feel that talk obstructs learning and actively discourage children's talk in school.
> Joan Tough, *Talk for Teaching and Learning*

Earlier in this book I tried to define and illustrate what learning-talk is. I then went on to assert that on the evidence we have, very little such talk takes place in schools. If this is true, and I believe it is, the result is that large numbers of children are being seriously disadvantaged in our schools by being cut off from their most natural and comfortable means of learning: talk. It is as if we teachers who control the language of education are ensuring that the learners do their learning in, as it were, a foreign language, a strange medium: reading, writing and passively listening. I believe, and this can only be an assertion, that this is an important underlying cause of a significant minority of children turning off for ever from education, and of a large number simply not achieving their potential. All children have the right to learn in the most appropriate and effective circumstances. This is a political issue.

Yet the Marxist argument that teachers are part of a middle-class plot to give the pupils (workers) sufficient education for them to be useful, but not enough for them to create a challenge, does not convince me. Teachers are thinking, sensitive and humane people who wish the pupils in their care to be successful. For the purposes of this book I ask you to share that assumption with me. We can then go forward to explore in detail why it is that talk for learning has not as yet assumed an important role in schools. Only through a careful, reasoned understanding of the problems and barriers surrounding the use of talk, and examination of the individual bricks in the wall, can we make progress towards creating a learning environment where talk takes its rightful place.

So far arguments have been angled at teachers as the ones chiefly responsible for all this. That may be true. But teachers teach children and they gain satisfaction from teaching them well. I have not yet met a teacher who would spurn an idea for making a lesson go more effectively or for making learning happen better. I believe that in the late 1970s a large number of teachers in the wake of the Bullock Report and the associated in-service thrusts really did try to use talk in their classrooms more regularly and found that they thereby created for themselves a number of new problems and inflamed some older difficulties. No doubt some of their efforts were misguided and naive. Better management and surer understanding could no doubt have lessened these difficulties but the first (and yet to be surmounted) barrier to using talk for learning was and still is the attitude of the children themselves to talk as a learning activity. Had the attempts teachers made in the 1970s to use talk in the classroom been received well by the learners then talk would, I believe, have flourished to the extent that it would not have been necessary to write this book.

So far this is all assertion and assumption lacking material evidence. During the autumn term of 1985, a Humanities teacher at a Leicestershire school, suggested to me that as part of my work in the family of schools I should undertake an investigation into pupils' attitudes to talk as a means of learning. The teacher and I devised and piloted a questionnaire to use amongst 50 12- and 13-year-old pupils (midway between the primary years and the exam-dominated years). The questionnaire was refined and adapted after a trial run, bearing in mind comments from the pupils. Our overall aim was to try to discover how the pupils felt about talk in comparison to other means of learning, to what extent they enjoyed it, and how well they felt they learned through talk. As it was necessary to include other means of learning in the survey we thereby gained a fascinating insight into how 50 children regarded different learning modes across the curriculum.

The questionnaire was talked through with the children as we went along and it was emphasised that they were considering the whole spectrum of learning in and out of school, and that 'learning' did not just mean learning facts but developing understanding, learning how to do things, developing in personal abilities and qualities. The first part (enjoyment) and the second part (learning best) were filled in separately by the pupils on different sides of the questionnaire, though for comparison purposes we present here the analysis of the results of both sections together.

The pupils were asked to make one of three possible responses to each item, one positive, one indeterminate and one hostile. Two supplementary questions were added: 'Which way of learning do you feel you get too much of in school?' and 'Which way of learning do you feel you don't get enough of?' In order to quantify results in our analysis we gave two points to a positive response, one point to an indeterminate response and no points to a negative response. Using this scoring system we were able to derive an overall score and a rank order for perceived enjoyment level and perceived learning level for each activity. The results are presented in Table 3.

Perhaps I should start with those activities which were popular on both enjoyment and learning counts. Watching/listening to TV/radio programmes, practical work and project work were the only activities to appear in the top four overall on both lists. Is this encouraging or not? Certainly the pupils thoroughly enjoyed practical work (though it was rated below writing on the 'learning' scale). It also got the highest score (14 responses) as the 'way of learning you feel you don't get enough of'. Follow-up discussion showed that by 'practical work' the pupils meant activities to do with real objects and materials (such as painting, cooking, craft work and science experiments) rather than, for example, making a play. This is encouraging for teachers trying to promote more active learning models.

How should we view the high rating for TV/radio programmes? Is it merely that the pupils felt entertained, and did no obvious work, or is it a tribute to the work of the TV companies in opening up the medium in a progressive way, tailoring programmes to teachers' needs and to modern classroom methodology? The response of the pupils to the question 'Which way of learning helps you to learn best?' was overall an honest one and I can only believe that they genuinely see such work as a positive learning experience.

During follow-up interviews we questioned pupils closely about project work; it emerged that a number of factors were at work in making it so popular and valued. It fitted into their overall view of learning which was generally to do with 'finding out something you've never known before'. However we as teachers might judge it, to the pupils the essence of the project work is finding out. Whilst having the variety pupils like and need to sustain interest ('it's nice doing different things on a project . . . reading, writing and drawing'), there is a strong base in the highly-valued activity of writing. Pupils also enjoyed the freedom and independence offered by project work: 'You can put what you want about it. When you're doing something in the whole class then you put what the teacher tells you to put, but when you're doing topic work, you've got a choice.' Glimmerings here of the pupils feeling a higher status as a learner in self-directed project work and having feelings of autonomy. Kevin hints at another understandable attraction – freedom of movement: 'Well, you can go up to the library – get books about it ... you're free to do what you want, really.'

Encouragingly, the pupils did not necessarily see the project as a lonely experience. 'I prefer it in groups ... 'cos there's more ideas. It's not just you in the group where the ideas are limited. You've got other people ... you combine your ideas and you can get a good project.'

It could be argued that watching TV and project work might be popular because they are undemanding, yet still seem to be respectable learning experiences. Nevertheless, we should give the pupils the benefit of the doubt about their views, and be encouraged by the findings that there are three major learning activities which pupils both enjoy and value.

Another pattern which can be seen in the results is that though the pupils did not really enjoy the 'traditional' classroom learning activities of reading, writing and listening to the teacher, they were rated more highly as ways of learning (see Table 3). Most significant here is the response to writing, which leapfrogs over practical work to third place on the 'learning best' scale. Yet 23 pupils complained that they got 'too much' writing in school. Evidently writing is valued for learning, but not enjoyed as teachers ask them to do far too much of it. Much the same could be said of 'listening to the teacher talk', which fifteen pupils complained they got 'too much of'.

Perhaps the most depressing result of all for those of us concerned to promote pupil talk in schools was that discussion work was not highly rated on either count. Whole-class discussion only just had the edge on 'listening to teacher explaining' (perhaps they emerge as the same thing in the minds of the pupils!). Small-group discussion, though mildly enjoyed as an activity, plummeted to bottom place as a valued learning activity.

In a follow-up questionnaire I asked pupils to make a direct comparison between whole-class discussion work and small-group work. The results are given in Table 4. Significant points from this are that pupils find small-group discussions a more relaxed and natural experience and find that they talk more and are marginally less dominated by one or two people doing all the talking. Yet in both contexts for discussion the majority of pupils complain that the activity is spoiled by some people messing about. This was the most common complaint expressed in the subsequent interviews and short pieces of writing we asked the pupils to do on the issue: 'Some people give stupid answers and play about ... people mess around and disturb everybody ...' The finding that pupils feel that they learn more in whole-class discussion is partly caused by their worries about control: at least in the whole-class discussion the teacher is there to try to do something

Table 3. Pupils' attitudes to methods of learning.

	Which way of learning do you enjoy or not?			Analysis of responses		Which way of learning helps you to learn best.			Analysis of responses		Which way of learning do you feel you get too much of in school?	Which way of learning do you feel you don't get enough of?
	Enjoy	OK	Dislike	Score	Rank order	I learn a lot	I learn something	I learn little	Score	Rank order		
1. Reading about the topic	2	39	11	43	7	14	33	5	61	5	5	1
2. Writing about the topic (essays/notes/answers to questions)	8	25	19	41	8	19	28	5	66	3	23	1
3. Doing practical work (making/experimenting)	42	8	2	92	1	19	26	7	64	4	0	14
4. A whole-class discussion where you give your ideas and listen to others	14	30	8	58	4	17	24	11	58	6	3	7
5. A small-group discussion where you give your ideas and listen to others	13	26	13	52	5=	12	15	25	39	10	1	1
6. Listening to the teacher explaining to the class and asking questions	10	15	27	35	10	13	30	9	56	7	15	0
7. Watching/listening to TV/radio programme	32	17	3	81	2	23	25	4	71	2	1	2
8. Asking other people questions	10	32	10	52	5=	9	29	14	47	9	0	1
9. Individual help, talking to the teacher	3	33	16	39	9	11	32	9	54	8	0	5
10. Doing a project on the topic	35	10	7	80	3	40	10	2	90	1	3	5

Table 4. Pupils' responses to discussion work.

	Small group	Whole class	Small group	Whole class
	Yes		No	
In discussions do you:				
Get embarrassed when you speak?	7	27	45	25
Say very little?	13	30	39	22
Do your fair share of talking?	40	26	12	26
Enjoy listening to what others have to say?	41	40	11	12
Often find that one or two people do all the talking?	29	41	23	11
Often lose concentration and stop listening?	19	29	33	23
Often find that some people spoil it by messing about?	37	40	15	12

about pupils who spoil things: 'You can all have a say and the teacher can keep order ... I prefer whole-group discussions because no one would be messing about because teacher has got their eye on them'. Simon says: 'If you are in a small group when you're with friends you tend to mess about more than you would if you were in a large group'.

The pupils expressed a number of reservations about whole-class discussion: 'the teacher keeps on talking about stuff which is boring' ... 'I get restless and lose concentration' ... 'it takes too long to get a say' ... 'they go on for ages' ... 'a class discussion doesn't achieve anything'. The crucially limiting factor about small-group discussions in the minds of the pupils was that they were too often disrupted by silly behaviour: 'Some people see [small-group] discussions as a chance to mess about' ... 'some people act silly without a teacher'.

Another common complaint was that, if they weren't being actively disrupted, small-group discussions often drifted away from the task in hand towards purposeless (value judgement) social gossip: 'they never talk about the subject' ... 'you sometimes drift away' ... 'Everybody starts talking about anything – what sort of trainers they've got and everything. It just moves away from the subject'.

Yet despite all the criticism of small-group discussion there was a strong undercurrent of feeling amongst the pupils interviewed that they appreciated and understood certain educational values in small-group discussions. Over half of them commented favourably on positive aspects of such work: 'You can do more talking' ... 'you can say what you think to your friends' ... 'you can speak without getting shy' ... 'you can get more talk in it and get it going' ... 'I like to give good ideas or to listen to them and to improve them by discussing'.

This last point – to do with the sharing of ideas and viewpoints – offered the most encouraging basis for discussion work. These pupils genuinely valued the chance to listen to other people's viewpoints in any discussion situation. Forty and 41 pupils in our survey said this about (respectively) whole-class and small-group discussions. This, of course, begs the question of whether they are consistently able to hear the views of others given the complaints about teacher domination and/or pupil misbehaviour. But there is surely something to build on here. The challenge for the teacher is to make discussion activities work for pupils. The evidence of the survey is that in the pupils' terms this means that: everyone should get a good share of discussion; the discussion should stick to the topic; and pupils shouldn't spoil things by messing about.

Our general impression was that these 12- and 13-year-old pupils had a very serious and responsible attitude to learning; there was only one frivolous or irresponsible answer by one boy who said he enjoyed small-group discussions because 'you can mess about'. So why is it that the pupils frequently complained about the failure of small-group discussions to achieve good learning? Why do they fly in the face of educational thought and rate it so lowly as a learning activity?

The following points emerged from the research. The first is to do with the image of learning that the pupils have. Despite our careful introduction the survey begged the question of what learning actually is. Semantically that word is perhaps a little loaded, in that it conjures up pictures of pupils sweating over lists, trying to 'learn' something by heart. My 11-year-old son, a product of an enlightened primary school and of parents anxious to promote a progressive view of education, told me 'learning is remembering'. In our follow-up interviews we were concerned to draw out the pupils' views on this. We found that these second- and third-year pupils, half-way through their secondary education, were completely consistent in their view of what learning is. Here are a selection of their responses to the question: 'What do you mean by "learning"?' 'Finding out something you didn't know' ... 'to find something new that you've never known before' ... 'finding out things' ... 'memorising things' ... 'knowing things' ... 'you might not understand something and then you get it explained to you and you've learned, you've understood something'.

At the heart of these comments (and there were many more like them) is an almost entirely transactional view of education. There is something that you are ignorant of, that the teacher (or the book, or the TV programme) knows about. The purpose of education is to somehow transfer that knowledge, that understanding, from the places it is stored to your head. Hence the weary putting-up with those monotonous tasks of reading, writing, listening to the teacher talk; they appear to the pupils as obvious and respectable means of the transmission of knowledge. Hence the approval of TV programmes and project work as they are so clearly connected with finding out information in a palatable (i.e. not boring) way. This is not to deny that learning has nothing to do with knowledge or understanding, only to say that many teachers have a different view to pupils of what knowledge and understanding is and how it is best achieved. These teachers would in the main stress other factors more strongly: the process of learning itself: the educational value, in terms of the growth of the individual, of the struggle to understand; the skills achieved during the journey towards the knowledge – finding out skills, talking skills, reading skills; the qualities that more pupil-centred and open-ended approaches can foster – independence, collaboration, autonomy. Teachers, too, would wish to start the journey at the point where the pupils are at, and rather than have them receive in a passive and detached way the knowledge and understanding from external sources, would seek to build on what is already perceived by the pupils and to encourage them to fit new insights into the emerging jigsaw in their hands. Hence the value that we teachers would place on discussion work, particularly small-group discussion work, as a means of sharing insights and of moving together towards fresh understanding. Pupils rate small group discussion work low as a learning activity as their picture of what learning is about is at odds with the progressive teacher's views. The following extract from a taped discussion illustrates the point:

Teacher: What do you think learning is?
Angela: General knowledge really.
Sarah: Looking at books and just learning.
Teacher: You don't rate drama as high as maths, then?
Various: No.
Angela: You can't really learn drama, can you, but you can learn different sums that you do in maths.
Teacher: You don't think you learn anything in drama?
Jessica: You learn *some* things ... you learn how to stage fight ...

This ties in with the views of other pupils who valued what they learned in activity-based subjects not in terms of the development of their own skills and powers of appreciation but as in terms of the knowledge acquired. Linda says of Music that she learns 'what different musical terms mean' and in PE and Drama 'you're finding out the correct sort of way to do certain things'. As a further denigration of activity-based subjects she says 'you don't need to know about how to play hockey for an O level ... but you might need to know about things like the Civil War ...'.

Believing that such a restricted view of learning was possibly a product of subject-based approaches at the secondary school, I asked 30 primary school pupils in the same family of schools what they thought learning was. The views were again entirely consistent with a transmission-of-content view: 'Learning is like someone teaching you and then you store it in your brain' ... 'Learning is storing bits of information in your brain in case you need it' ... 'Learning is listening, finding out, or being told what to do' ... 'Learning is reading, English, Fletcher [a Maths textbook]'.

Ten-year-old Phillipa was asked what she felt about a piece of small-group extended discussion work which the whole class had thoroughly enjoyed and which the teachers had judged to be highly successful in terms of the skills and the confidence generated. She commented:

> I'm sort of in the middle ... I'd liked to have got on with my work, yet I was pleased to do this, so I'm kind of in the middle about it ... it was a good idea up to a certain extent. I thought it would have been probably better if we'd have got on with ... a lot more reading because I particularly want to catch up with my Fletcher ...

Discussion, evidently is not to do with work, or learning.

The second key point flows from the above, and concerns the image the pupils have of themselves as learners in relation to the teacher. Because the pupils have a view of learning as a closed, content-based activity, they do not feel that they can learn much from each other. It is only the teacher, the text book, the TV programme that hold the knowledge. Consequently learning cannot happen in small pupil-based groups, as the teacher is not there to control both the behaviour of the group and to transmit the knowledge. The following extract from an interview with Carol is very revealing.

> *Carol:* If you've got a big-group discussion you've usually got a teacher leading it, so it's easier so he or she might bring the discussion on by asking questions and everyone gets a turn; but in little-group discussions, you've perhaps not got a teacher always with you and people start to mess about and it doesn't seem to work as well.
>
> *Teacher:* Is that in all subjects?
>
> *Carol:* We have good [whole-class] discussions in English ... Mr Lewis likes leading it and can ask good questions but if you have little groups, he's perhaps not always there ... and if you're talking about something ... if you want to learn something, you've got to know the right answer ... and if you're in little groups, you've perhaps not got the teacher with you to tell you that you're right or wrong about something ...

If learning has a 'right answer' which the pupils have 'got to know', then it is no wonder that small-group discussion, whose main value is seen by educationalists as to do with collaboration, self-expression, exploration, is undervalued by the pupils. The teacher, or the book, telling you what you need to know, short circuits all this lengthy and demanding process of discussion.

The view of learning as having a 'right answer' accounts in turn for the fact that so many small-group discussions appear to be spoiled by people messing about. The expression of ideas and views by peers is not important as it will not deliver the knowledge. Hence the complaints of pupils laughing at others who try to take the work seriously. 'In the small groups ... if you come out with something the boys seem to laugh at you and say that, that's stupid ...'. Presumably, in the whole-class discussions a teacher can try to protect pupils from this kind of experience.

Another curious finding from the survey and research is explained by this content-based 'right and wrong' view of learning. There were consistent complaints in the interviews and the writing about 'arguing' in discussion work spoiling things. If the pupils see the aim of discussion work as deciding on a right answer, rather than as a way of exploring and developing ideas collaboratively, then a new polarity is added to the teenagers' tendency to be argumentative and to stand up for their views. Evidently many of the pupils found this disturbing: 'Some people get carried away and you can't agree and just start arguing ... I don't like people to argue ... we don't agree ... we very often fall out ... everybody shouts and you don't get anywhere ... I don't like arguing with my friends.'

Amongst teenage pupils it is my feeling that this tendency not to take each other seriously is compounded by their own increasing self-consciousness and their view of authority. It is not 'cool' for a teenager to co-operate too obviously and closely with a teacher's approaches. This can in extreme forms manifest itself in overtly anti-social behaviour, but most pupils would not particularly wish to rebel or disrupt; they are just a little self-conscious about appearing as a serious, co-operative learner when amongst peers and out of the eye of the teacher. The presence of one wit in a small group ready to comment ironically on any offered views which set themselves up by virtue of their seriousness or tentative nature, can seriously inhibit discussion.

One other interesting point occurs. There were 27 girls and 25 boys in our sample. Initially the breakdown of results was done on a sex basis. Interestingly, in this sample, where the number of boys and girls was roughly equal, the results were nearly identical. Similar numbers of boys and girls did or did not get embarrassed in whole- and small-class discussion, and felt that they did 'their fair share of talking'. These results would seem to challenge the conventional wisdom that girls are dominated by boys in the discussion; indeed we were encouraged by the complaint from one plaintive male: 'the teacher lets the girls do all the talking'.

If this sample of pupils is in any way typical it is apparent that their view of learning is an important, perhaps crucial, element in the success or otherwise of talk in the classroom. It would help if we could firmly establish how and why those views were formed. Presumably we can point the finger at the teacher again. Where else do you learn about learning other than in school? Everywhere, of course. What image of learning is presented by society as a whole? The media certainly has a key role here. Comics inevitably show a transmission view of learning: the teacher stands at the front (wearing a mortarboard) and tells the pupils things. Whenever schools are in the news, the item is preceded by TV pictures of pupils in serried ranks poring over books as the teacher points to the blackboard and expounds the subject. The odd shy hand is raised in response to closed-seeming questions. What price learning-talk in this environment? The most learned people presented on television or radio are those exemplified by such programmes as *Mastermind* and *Brain of Britain* where the scale of learning is directly related to the amount of factual information on obscure subjects the participants can cram into their heads at one time. Parents, too, are undoubtedly a powerful influence. We judge the learning process in terms of the way we were taught and in that way the models of 20 years ago are effortlessly transferred to the next generation.

But I am not qualified nor do I have space here to do more than speculate about general social effects. What is more important for my purposes is that it must surely be true that children's experience of school is a powerful ingredient in the forming of their attitudes to learning activities. We must therefore conclude that, whatever the teacher's overt intentions may be, the learners are receiving the message from school that learning is a matter of the transition of content from 'them as knows' to 'them as don't know', through the means of reading, writing, listening and thereby memorising. If fruitful learning-talk is as rare as I have claimed in the last chapter we could argue that the pupils can hardly value such talk if they have seldom encountered it.

Pupil attitudes, however formed, are a powerful constraint on the use of talk in schools. What other factors, pressures and constraints serve to squeeze out pupil talk from the official classroom agenda?

During 1985–6 I worked with a number of different groups of teachers on in-service courses examining the role of talk in the classroom. I asked each of these separate groups of teachers to 'brainstorm' ideas about the reasons for the underuse of talk. Here is a rationalised compilation of what they came up with:

Noise
Furniture
Need to be seen to be coping
Control
Pupils do not respond
Pupils do not take each other seriously
Slow and roundabout method

Examination syllabuses demand more formal work
Difficult to monitor
Difficult to assess
Parental opposition
Heads prefer traditional modes of learning
Teachers not sure of purposes
Promotion
Too risky

Let us take a closer look at that list, starting with the most obvious and surface aspect – the physical environment.

Most classrooms are not ideal breeding grounds for pupil talk. If the children are to talk to and with each other they need to be able to hear each other clearly. They can't do this whilst sitting in serried ranks; the easiest and most obvious person to hear in this environment is the teacher who is usually standing up and can thereby project his or her voice all over the classroom. I have noticed how teachers have a habit of repeating what pupils say, as the following extract from a whole-class discussion shows:

Teacher: Why might the tin buckle up in this way?
Anne: Because the sides are sucked in?
Teacher: Because the sides are sucked in. Yes that's one idea. Any more?
David: Because it overheated.
Teacher: Yes it might have overheated.
Peter: Because it got crushed by the air pressure.
Teacher: It got crushed by the air pressure. Can you explain that?

Is this habit of repetition born of the teacher's desire to dominate events? I believe that the answer is much simpler; it came to me during a day when I was shadowing a pupil: sitting at desk level there are usually several bodies between you and the pupil-speaker – bodies which have an uncomfortable habit of breathing, coughing, shuffling about. In the average class discussion it is very difficult indeed to hear what your classmates are saying. The teacher reacts, almost instinctively, by becoming a sort of time-lapsed megaphone, loudspeaking the comments of the pupils. It is possible to overcome these difficulties with whole-class discussion and I shall later suggest specific strategies for doing so.

If a teacher wants to break up this pattern the furniture is not always adaptable or easily moved so that pupils can sit round in smaller groups. In some schools moving furniture is a political act. I collected the following from a classroom door in Bristol:

In no circumstances are the desks and tables in this room to be moved.
Albert Bloggs, Deputy Head.

It would seem that there are teachers laying claim to 'ownership' of rooms who see the act of moving desks as a violation of their personal space – a threat to their survival kit. I can understand this though I do not approve of it. Used to having a teacher's desk and a U-shaped arrangement of desks myself, I try to make this the arrangement in classes I teach in. It is a context I feel safe and happy in. When other teachers spoil it by swapping the desks round I get annoyed. It is as if another teaching model has come in to threaten and oust my own. Patterns of classroom layout are therefore political in their implications. I suspect the deputy head's notice was not just an indication that someone had left the desks in disorder. It implied that the desks were not to be moved *in any circumstances* whether you put them back or not; we are not having any of this progressive nonsense *here*.

Even if the desks are movable and flexible, classrooms are still not places where it is easy to talk. Bare floors and walls echo and distort sound, the talk of other groups distracts and causes the noise level to rise so that you have to talk over others to be heard and then they have to talk louder to hear each other ... On in-service courses, where we are split into groups we inevitably seek our own personal space, insulated from other groups if possible, preferably in a separate area. Rarely do we tolerate more than two groups to a room. The odds are stacked against classroom talk from the start.

And what about all that noise generated by talk? It is not just that teachers physically cannot tolerate certain decibel levels. There's more to it.

There are enormous pressures on teachers to be 'in control'. The first comes from within. Teaching is a stressful occupation. In one sense your personality is laid on the line throughout the day and for secondary teachers in seven or eight different circumstances each day. The motivation which overwhelms one in these circumstances is nothing to do with education: it is simply to get through the day more or less intact. I have known teachers to brood about a bad Friday all weekend. One difficult class can sour your whole week, can sap you even when you are not with them. Teachers want their lessons to be calm, orderly events. It takes a great deal of energy, commitment and hope to take risks in the school day and talk can be a risky business. If in a silent reading period a few children are not reading then they can sit there and turn pages and stare at the book without wrecking the lesson. The same is true of writing. Children are absolute experts at playing the teacher's games whilst making the minimum of demands on their own resources. There sometimes seems to be an unspoken contract implied in secondary classrooms: you do not make too many demands on us and we will keep more or less orderly. But you cannot do that with talk. Talk is a very up-front, public activity. If a whole-class discussion is going wrong, or is being wrecked by a few individuals, the humiliation of the teacher is there for all to see. If small groups are fooling about or, worst of all, just not talking at all, everyone knows about it. The teacher is naked in his or her failure and thereby is tempted to clothe it with the less exposed activity of reading, writing, topic work (perhaps letting them chatter while they are doing it). Pupil talk poses a threat to teachers' ability to cope.

The evidence from the teachers I talk to is that these sorts of things are noticed in the wider arena. The word 'promotion' on the list puzzled me for a while. Why should using classroom talk used in the way recommended consistently by educational theorists, advisers, HMI and the DES hinder career prospects? The answer links other aspects of my lists of constraints together. It is the clear impression of teachers that credibility in school amongst pupils, fellow teachers and the school hierarchy is determined largely by your perceived ability to cope and be in control. Heads taking visitors around beam in approval at a class working quietly and busily at reading or writing. They feel less sure about groups of children engaging in noisy role-play or vigorous, animated small-group discussion. This, despite the lipservice they pay to the notions of encouraging the active participation of children. Secondary heads are particularly prone to this creeping control disease. Good teaching and learning is seen as a matter of teacher being in command, and command is assessed by answers to the most superficial question: are the children quiet and seemingly busy? It was so refreshing to be shown round a primary school on one memorable occasion by a head who took me into a lower junior class where the hum was so busy, that he had to raise his voice to comment to me: 'Great! It almost looks like education doesn't it?' Another teacher I spoke to, the head of department of a small secondary school, felt that his credibility amongst fellow teachers in his department had been endangered since he had switched the emphasis in his classroom towards the pupils' active participation in talk. You cannot hear writing or reading lessons down the corridor. If a talk lesson is going well, you are likely to hear it several rooms away and it will draw a corridor-stalking deputy like a magnet.

In this situation no service is done to the cause of talk by teachers (there is one in every school) who hide behind the rhetoric of talk philosophy to rationalise sheer sloppy teaching. One of the illusions I hope to dispel in this book is that to enable pupil learning-talk to thrive in the classroom you have to throw all the rules out of the window and just let the pupils do what they want. Successful classroom talk requires an entirely different (and ultimately more important) kind of discipline and involves a new and more meaningful 'contract' between the teacher and the learners. The learners must understand that the invitation to participate is in fact an opportunity to take responsibility for their own learning. The teacher in turn has the responsibility of doing his or her best to ensure that the learning takes place successfully. That means that pupils bawling out of windows, or sitting round in corners comparing the price of their training shoes, or the comparative attractiveness of the boys or girls in the classroom must not be rationalised as letting their ideas flow, or communicating in any way that is remotely educational. Teachers who have led themselves to believe that such activities and such classrooms are contributing to the learning process are endangering the credibility and the health of genuine learning-talk in schools, not least in the eyes of the learners themselves. No, successful learning-talk requires a relaxed, two-way environment, but it also needs careful preparation, a disciplined and purposeful atmosphere and a teacher who knows good learning when he or she sees it.

In this connection it is worth mentioning that many teachers may not know good talk when they hear it because they are unconvinced by the value of pupil talk in the first place. Wells and Wells (1984) claim that the most serious impediment to the use of talk in schools is 'a less than wholehearted belief by many teachers in the value that pupil talk has for learning'. They go on to explain this by saying that 'many of us had years of being *talked at* as pupils and students and have probably unconsciously absorbed the belief that, as teachers, we are not doing our job properly unless we are talking – telling, questioning or evaluating' DES (1979 p. 94).

> Although considerable research over the last twenty years into the ways in which language is acquired and extended has emphasised the part that talking can play in learning, the evidence of the survey indicates that this is still not widely known amongst teachers.

It would appear that teachers want to remain firmly in control of the agenda for learning and thus talk opportunities are squeezed out.

Several of the items on the list produced by those teacher groups point towards the content of lessons being a major constraint on the use of talk. The secondary school examination board syllabuses lay down that a certain amount of ground must be covered and the teachers must keep to this. Where the content element is heavy, talk appears to be a long-winded and slow process by which to proceed. Teachers are tempted to take short cuts. The quickest is simply to issue the notes, the facts, raw. In many ways I am seduced by the idea of doing this and then using the resulting acres of released time for real learning. But teachers prefer to have the content processed just a little – through the chalk and talk sessions and the 'finding-out' worksheets. Inevitably the teachers complain that if it were not for the domination of examination content they could go about the business of teaching in a much more open and educational way. However, we cannot entirely blame exams for choking up education with content and thus squeezing out talk. I have heard the same excuses offered by teachers of classes unconstrained by exam outcomes, including those in primary schools. Teachers cling with a curious mixture of resentment and nostalgia to the notion that there is certain 'stuff' that has to be got through so that the next stage of education can be approached successfully. My son was told by his English teacher in the second year of secondary school that he had to learn parts of speech in order to pass his O level. Parts of speech was dropped many years ago from the syllabus he will encounter at 16. Now O level has finally bowed out to be replaced by the more process-based GCSE syllabuses, the teacher will have to turn to a different constraint to justify learning parts of speech; I am confident that the mental agility will be there to find it.

So teachers would seem to cling on to notions of learning being a matter of conveying content-based courses as this is one convenient way of keeping control of classroom behaviour by maintaining tight control of the agenda for learning itself: 'Now come on . . . we've got a lot to get through today'. The teacher is the person who decides what is to be learned, devises ways of the 'stuff' being learned, monitors the procedure and assesses how much has been learned.

These last two elements, monitoring and assessment, would seem to present further stumbling blocks for teachers seeking to use learning-talk as an everyday part of classroom activity. Again the underlying question is one of control. Teachers have a need to be in control in the obvious disciplinary sense, and they wish, too, to control the agenda for learning and the way that agenda proceeds in the classroom. That means they want to know what is going on, not in any sinister way, but because they are sincere (if at times misguided) professionals anxious to see that their job is being done. When the pupils are talking this causes difficulty for teachers.

It would seem to be a relatively easy matter to monitor and assess the value of whole-class discussion. I have heard a teacher say of a discussion session 'I know in my guts it was right'. We can all feel if a whole-class session has gone well or not; but there are underlying doubts. Any whole-class discussion is largely dominated by a few individuals. Is our valuing of such a discussion simply a response to the contribution of a few pupils? And what of the others? What is the value for them? Are they participating in any sense? Are they indeed listening at all? I am reminded of my posture at lectures in my university days, chin on hand, staring with intent and curious gaze at the man in front of me from whose mouth emerged strings of words like so much bunting. Meanwhile my mind was free to wander in its garden of lust.

The problem becomes more difficult when the teacher is trying to monitor small-group discussions. All those pupils chattering away. What are they saying? What is happening when they laugh? Children do laugh a lot when they are working together. You have little chance of keeping tabs yourself and do not have enough tapes or recorders, sockets, extension leads or batteries to be able to keep a taped record. Even if you do you can hardly hear what is going on for all the noise, and a half-hour tape of one group takes an hour to listen to properly and several more hours to transcribe. I am troubled when I hear non-teachers suggesting to teachers that they regularly make transcripts of group discussions and use them as a basis for evaluating performance. What do they think teachers *do* all night long?

Suppose we do have the opportunity to eavesdrop personally or electronically on discussions and suppose we do manage to decipher, roughly, what is being said and who is saying it; what do we make of what we hear? Interpreting the learning going on in small-group discussion is an art based on a clear understanding of the theory and plenty of experience of the practice. We might be able to hear the voices on the surface but it is another matter to be able to detect the underlying currents of learning.

So it is no wonder that writing is a safer, easier medium to deal with even though educationalists' perceptions of what good writing is and what writing can do have become more complex and confused in recent years, whereas the consensus about talk is, as I have tried to show, much clearer. You know where you stand with pen and paper. You can put it in neat piles in your briefcase, monitor it at home at times convenient to you. What takes half an hour to write can be assessed with confidence in a matter of minutes, and if the content of it is dubious you can always rely on spelling and handwriting to make your judgements. No wonder teachers are reluctant to make that leap in the dark.

In these circumstances the status quo always starts as favourite. Unless teachers are very sure of their purposes, are confident of their perceptions of what constitutes good learning, they are likely to remain timid about making that necessary shift in classroom methodology to enable talk to take its rightful place.

There are, therefore, powerful barriers to constrain and limit the use of learning-talk in the classroom. The rest of this book will endeavour to explore ways in which we can try to overcome or minimise those constraints once they have been acknowledged.

PART FOUR
Finding the right context for talk

7 Exploring the arenas

You have a group of 30 children for an hour. You have acknowledged all the constraints and difficulties and are still prepared to make the necessary act of faith to set up some situations in which talk is the natural means of learning. What do you ask them to do and do you ask them to do it in pairs, small groups or whatever? And is whole-class discussion inevitably an inappropriate arena for learning-talk, as has been suggested in some parts of this book? Teachers have plenty of ideas of *what* they would like children to be talking about; it is the *how* and *where* that cause the problems.

In this chapter I shall begin by exploring what I feel small groups can achieve which is difficult to achieve in larger, more public situations. With the background of my own distrust and suspicion of the whole-class arena I shall then go on to suggest strategies teachers can nevertheless use to make for more successful learning-talk in larger groups. I shall do this by offering you two more stories from which I attempt to draw conclusions. Your conclusions will and should be different to mine, because the children you teach and the schools you teach in are different. The most I can hope to offer are clues.

The Humanities class I was teaching in 1983 seemed a very nice group of young people. They were now half-way through their fifth year and I had taught them since Christmas of their fourth year. Mixed-ability classes depend crucially on the chemistry of classroom relationships and interaction. This one was working well. Students worked a lot together, got on well, though there could be lively disagreements. Quite simply, they seemed to like being together.

I had to push the group quite hard about written work; they had understood that I saw it as a necessary, if not welcome, part of the assessment process. But the talk flowed easily and well. We would often spend upwards of half an hour in a completely relaxed way, talking through things as a whole class, letting the discussion lead us wherever it strayed.

On one particular day in early spring the discussion touched on an area we'd never previously explored: ethnic minorities. The school was in West Leicestershire, but was unfortunately not significantly enriched by the strong multi-ethnic communities living in and around Leicester itself. We had two Asian boys in the class who were generally very popular.

I do not remember clearly how the discussion reached this point but suddenly these seemingly humane and enlightened students began to make statements that were highly racist in tone and implication – so much so that I believed at first that they were not being serious and that this was instead a sophisticated parody of such views: 'They are all on the dole – taking all the country's money' . . . 'They come over here and take all our jobs' . . . 'It's not fair; they ought to send them all home'. These and other ludicrous contradictions received no challenge. What does a teacher do with all this? I had never taken a direct anti-racist line before as young people are highly resistant to moral pressure from adults in authority; but I found myself doing so now. Desperately I looked for allies but could see nothing but nodding faces and hear nothing but the silence of tacit acceptance of the racist views being expressed.

This experience shook me for some time. As one who believes that the vast majority of children are innately humane and thinking beings, I found that belief now undermined. Here was a group of seemingly enlightened and warm-hearted 15-year-olds who got on well together, who worked daily with two very well-liked Asian peers, but who were under the surface dangerously racist. My attempts at educating them had not succeeded one jot in leading them out from themselves towards a better understanding of the world and other people. This was one of the best groups I had ever taught. At that moment I could have cheerfully left teaching. I felt I had been fighting a losing battle and I was not sure if it was going to be a lot of fun trying to win.

Four weeks later came an experience which put all this in perspective. As part of their examination coursework assessment, the students were permitted to submit up to two pieces on tape. This had encouraged a number of them to set up and record small-group discussions around chosen issues. The class understood that if they got their act together, found a spare room, cassette and tape recorder they could have permission at any time to go away and talk together. My only rule that once the tape had started, they left it running and left the pause button alone. In this way I could listen to the whole discussion, warts and all, rather than to over-rehearsed slices of it. Anne, Julie, Sue and Teresa asked me that day whether they could make a tape on animal rights. Half an hour later they came back and handed me the tape. Anne said guiltily: 'You haven't to take any notice of the argument halfway through: we went off the topic a bit'. That evening I reviewed the tape. It was an example of a good, collaborative discussion. The girls had explored a number of issues in a thoughtful and supportive way. About half-way through the tape they were talking about pets disappearing in doubtful circumstances. Were they being kidnapped for vivisection? Then came the following extract: Julie had been waiting some time to get her oar in:

1 *Julie:*   Can I speak now, please?
2 *Sue:*   If you want.
3 *Julie:*   You know Leicester, right? My uncle lives there and he's got this dog and he got it off us like, right. And it were only a small dog ... it were only a pup and it went missing ... and we thought ... well some Pakis lived down the road and we reckon they've ate it.
4 *Sue:*   The dog?
5 *Julie:*   Yes.
6 *Anne:*   No ... don't be so ...
7 *Sue:*   Oh my God!
8 *Julie:*   It went missing and they looked everywhere.
9 *Anne:*   How could they prove it?
10 *Julie:*   They can't.
11 *Sue:*   Yes, but it's there?
12 *Anne:*   Why does it have to be them?
13 *Sue:*   Yeah, that's ... that's ... um (clicks fingers).
14 *Anne:*   I'm doing my special enquiry on racism – that is *racist*.
15 *Julie:*   Yeah it is.
16 *Anne:*   That is ... you accuse them, I mean where is ... they're probably English ... it don't matter about the colour ... I mean ... just.
17 *Julie:*   I'm not saying it was the colour.
18 *Sue:*   . Yeah, you know it could have been anybody who took it to eat it.
19 *Anne:*   Yes, exactly. It could have got knocked down.
20 *Sue:*   It could have got knocked down – it could have been put in the hedge or something. Could have been took away to one of those farms, you know, where they kill them.
21 *Anne:*   Yes, you're saying that you think it's the Pakis who ...
22 *Sue:*   You're racialist.
23 *Julie:*   (*screaming*) No, I'm *not*.
24 *Sue:*   You are.
25 *Julie:*   I'm *not*.
26 *Anne:*   Don't shout.
27 *Julie:*   No.
28 *Sue:*   You are, because you said that they're coloured who'd eaten it.
29 *Julie:*   I says it could have been.
30 *Sue:*   Yes, but you're still saying it could have been.
31 *Anne:*   Yeah, I mean it could have been the *white* people.
32 *Julie:*   It could have been, yeah.
33 *Sue:*   You didn't say that though did you? No! See? Come on Teresa, say something.
             (*Pause*)
34 *Sue:*   Oh, you're not racist as well are you?

35 *Teresa:* No.

36 *Julie:* I ain't anyway.

37 *Anne:* I know, but it sounded it the way you said it.

38 *Sue:* I know ... but you hear about all those rabbits that go missing ... and the police and that and whoever ... they complain that it's the coloureds that take it.

39 *Anne:* The coloureds get the blame for everything.

40 *Sue:* I know, but if we say to somebody you're racialist ... you go up to somebody and say 'you're racialist' ...

41 *Anne:* They say 'oh, I'm not'.

42 *Sue:* Say it's a cop or something ... you'll get really done for it ... but if a cop comes up to you and says 'you're racialist', then we'd get done for it.

43 *Julie:* Yeah, but that's going off the subject.

44 *Sue:* No, it's not ...

45 *Julie:* ... to ... coloureds then ...

46 *Anne:* I know ... I'm in the same form as Harbo and Was and that and they're a great laugh ... they're really nice ... and my dad works with these coloureds and he says they're the best workers in the factory. They're the only ones that work. The others sit and talk.

47 *Julie:* The only reason why the whites call blacks is because ...

48 *Anne:* Jealous.

49 *Julie:* Yes because they've got jobs and we haven't.

50 *Anne:* They've got jobs ... they work.

51 *Julie:* Because they've come into our country and they've got qualifications and take our jobs.

52 *Anne:* Like this. I had an argument with this lad. He said that they should get rid of all the blacks ... I says, yeah, you get rid of all the blacks in Leicester and how many firms will go bankrupt ... how many people will be out of jobs ... (*supportive noises from Sue*) ... they've got all the factories and they employ white people.

53 *Sue:* If they went, nobody would know where they're going or anything.

54 *Anne:* We employ ... there's not many white people that employ coloureds ... but if they do they find out that they work harder than all the whites.

55 *Sue:* But there's a lot of coloureds that employ white people though, isn't there?

56 *Anne:* You find that it's really different ...

57 *Sue:* Anyway ... back to animals.

Since this tape recording was instrumental in my recovering a certain faith in the educational process in schools, it perhaps merits a closer look.

Julie has come out with a highly racist mouthful – the kind of statement that a month before had passed completely unchallenged in the whole-class discussion. But this time the reaction of the others in the group is hearteningly different. At first they express incredulity: 'don't be so ... Oh my God!' (6, 7). Anne and Sue then ask important questions: 'How could they prove it?' (9) ... 'Why does it have to be them?' (12) and move on to downright indignation and condemnation of what they see as something morally and factually unacceptable: 'that is *racist*' (14) ... 'You're racialist' (22). The anger and sense of outrage here is genuine. Julie's first response is to deny everything (unfairly): 'I says it could have been' (29) and then to claim that she isn't racist: 'I ain't anyway' (36). The group then recovers its good nature and goes on to a more relaxed exploration of ideas in which Sue reveals some disturbing underlying assumptions and Julie reverts to type: 'They've got jobs and we haven't' (49). It is at this stage of the discussion that Anne asserts herself through a number of powerful statements about her own feelings and experiences. Her force is the most powerful influence. She wins the overlying argument and has every chance, I judge, of influencing Julie's inner core of belief. A similar public challenge from a teacher may well have proved counterproductive and served to harden up beliefs and polarise positions. In my most cynical moments I believe that the quickest way to get children to do or think something is to tell them *not* to. A survey in Wales in 1986 of young people's attitudes towards authority figures showed that teachers topped the untrustworthiness league with 40 per cent of the votes amongst girls, whereas amongst the boys, teachers were only marginally more trustworthy than politicians and were on a par with the police. Teachers seeing themselves as a direct source of moral authority should ponder this point carefully. A parallel for teachers would be to imagine that a lesson had been observed by a close colleague and by an HMI. Whose comments would carry more weight in terms of influencing future practice? If you share my belief in the fundamental good nature of young people, then you will perhaps share my belief that the peer group is a powerful context for change and development.

Yet a month earlier the peer group norms had seemed to accept and endorse blatant racism. What was the difference and why had Anne not spoken up then? I was forced to re-examine the earlier discussion in the light of this tape recording. A month ago, however gentle the nature of the class, the discussion had been a public one. Who had done the talking? I had been aware of half an hour's vigorous if unpalatable discussion. On reflection I could think of four boys who had made the vast majority of contributions and several other students who had chipped in from time to time. No more than a third of the class had actually spoken. I talked to Anne about this. Why had not she spoken out earlier: 'It's not worth it,' she said, 'they don't really think that anyway'.

I had a powerful sense that what had been happening on that earlier discussion was that street norms had taken over. By that I imply that there are certain overtly public norms that seem to be powerful amongst young

people in gaining street credibility. These norms seem to be largely associated with males and have a distinctly anti-progressive tone and macho
flavour. It would not do and it is not cool to cross them in public. The more
public the situation the more the norms seem to harden up. So this group
of four girls can be honest in revealing their feelings and ideas to each other.
There is an atmosphere of trust which encourages the open revelation
of feelings and ideas. This is a powerful disagreement but one which takes
place on 'safe ground' between friends, and all is forgiven at the end.

In the whole-group, 'public' situation, much more was at stake. Contributions were not made 'face to face' within touching and smelling
distance of each other, but from separate areas of a spread-out classroom.
There was, as in all class discussions, an impersonal, risky feel; a touch of
aggression. This was no place for the supportiveness and tentative flavour
of an exploratory discussion. Here was an arena where your colours were
laid out and they had better be acceptable. It occurs to me that the small
groups provide a context which will enable different kinds of discussion
because there is a different frame of reference, a different set of expectations
about the sort of talking that goes on. The discussion about handicapped
children referred to in Chapter 4 had allowed the students to explore
feelings and ideas that would be well nigh impossible to expose in the
whole class where different norms seem to operate.

The experience prompted me to approach our annual new parents'
evening in a different way. In the past, three of us had talked in turn from
the platform and received questions from assembled groups of 200–300
parents. The atmosphere and questioning had usually tended towards the
hostile: 'Why don't you set more homework?' and 'I'm glad to see you
gentlemen are wearing ties. Can't you persuade your colleagues to do so?'

The following year we put the parents into groups of ten or twelve
with two teachers. An atmosphere of open, sharing discussion based on
thoughtful questions was reported by everyone. More people had talked,
which was obvious, but a much higher proportion of women had seemed
to contribute. I have as yet no firm evidence for this, but it appears to me
that if we are seeking to explore ways in which girls and women can take
a fuller part in their own education we need to provide alternative contexts
to the whole-group discussion which so often defers to the unwritten rules
of 'boys' games'.

Two years later came an opportunity to look further into this. I had
observed a Humanities class at a similar stage in their education to my
class referred to above. The topic under consideration was immigration.
There had been a promising start to the lesson; a label had been stuck on
each pupil's back giving their fictitious name, ethnic origin, time and reason
of emigration to England. In the warm-up exercise they had had to find
out who they were and all about their circumstances by asking others who
could read what was on their backs. The whole class then re-formed, pupils

introduced themselves and an open discussion started. Before long the familiar, unacceptable comments were frothing out, laced by one or two worthy of prosecution under the Race Relations Act. The teacher and I grew irritated and assertive. This seemed to provoke a further round of even more blatant comments from a certain dominant section of boys. The girls by and large hung their heads and shuffled their feet uneasily.

The following lesson I asked three from this particular group of boys who had seemed so keen in public to give vent to their racist views whether they would be prepared to discuss the issue further in a smaller group. Almost anything is preferable to 'work' and they enthusiastically agreed. I provided a few questions as prompters in case they needed them (for example, 'Do you feel it is a good thing or a bad thing to have a wide racial mix in a country like Britain?') but they only referred to them briefly towards the beginning of the discussion. I joined them at the beginning and end of the discussion; otherwise they were completely on their own. Here are some interesting (and representative) sections of the 25-minute tape they produced:

1 *Mick:* (*Reading*) 'Do you feel it is a good thing to have a wide racial mix in a country like Britain?'

2 *Alan:* Yeah ... get to know about other sort of cultures and ...

3 *Seb:* Yeah ... it's partly 50/50 because ...

4 *Mick:* I wouldn't mind having a few less of them here, you know.

5 *Alan:* A few less of them!

6 *Seb:* People think ... people from Leicester, white people, think that there's a lot of blacks, but they all hang around in Leicester, that's why ... Birmingham and things like that. They all sort of hang around in the Midlands, so you take it for granted that they're all over the place, but really it's only Leicester and Birmingham and places like that.

7 *Alan:* You say ... put 'em ... let 'em go back home. But you can't make 'em go back home if this *is* their home they were born in, can you?

8 *Mick:* Yeah ... and a lot of people, they don't like their home. That's why they moved here.
     (*Later*)

9 *Mick:* I know this half-caste kid who lives in London and, er, he does ... I like him, he's a good kid, but some of them, you know, Reggae and all that ... the Rastafarians who talk like blinkin Jamaicans ... I don't see the point in that, really.

10 *Seb:* Some Jamaicans are all right. Like I know this kid called Irvin Miles.

11 *Mick:* Yeah ... I know him.

12 *Seb:* He used to be in Charnwood. He was a laugh.

13 *Alan:* A right peasant!

14 *Mick:* No, but I think, yeah, going back to the peasants, wogs and coons and that, I think that's unfair ... I mean ...

15 *Seb:*   I mean they call us when we're in their country.

16 *Mick:*   White people *are* peasants, some of them, aren't they?

17 *Alan:*   Yeah.

18 *Seb:*   They get mad when we call them peasants and wogs and niggers and things like that, but they call us honkies don't they?

19 *Mick:*   I've never heard a black kid call anybody a honky.

20 *Alan:*   But we don't live in a place where there's loads of blacks.

21 *Mick:*   Yeah, I've been to Birmingham plenty of times, though.

22 *Seb:*   Like, I've been through Leicester, when I was down the primary school. We went on a walk through Leicester ... looking at all the old back-to-back houses and everything like that ... and we went through Highfields and there was a big, sort of ... what are they called ? ... big sort of church.

23 *Mick:*   Temple.

24 *Seb:*   And they were all littered on the roads and everything.

25 *Mick:*   What? Black people?

26 *Seb:*   Sikhs ... or Hebrews ... and things like that ...

27 *Mick:*   I don't like Sikhs, though.

28 *Seb:*   And we walked by and they started picking stones up and throwing them at us and we all had to run ... because we were supposed to be stopping and sketching this cathedral thing, but they all started throwing stones at us and shouting in their language and we all run, because we couldn't do anything about it ...

29 *Mick:*   It's partly because ... er ... if ... like ... we call them coons and that and that's how they wanna ...

30 *Alan:*   Get us back.

31 *Mick:*   Get us back, like.

32 *Seb:*   Yes, but we were only about eight or nine and they were adults and they were throwing at juniors.

33 *Mick:*   Well, you see, it don't make much difference, really ... because they'll just pick on anybody.

34 *Alan:*   It's stupid.

35 *Mick:*   I know it's stupid, but they'll pick on any white kid to get revenge, you know, even if it is a nine-, ten-year-old.
(*Later*)

36 *Mick:*   I don't mind people being racist, but when they ...

37 *Seb:*   Keep quiet about it ... but when they go round causing trouble ...

38 *Alan:*   What about that march a couple of days ago? That is *stupid*, that is ... going on a march because you don't like black people.

39 *Mick:*   I think ... sometimes I feel sorry ... because one time when I went to Birmingham I was just walking along with my mum and dad, and a load of white kids were on the other side of this street and there's two of these black kids, Jamaicans walking up the same side but the other way, and these white kids just started picking on them and calling them coons and that ... I feel sorry for them when they start going to that extent.

40 *Seb:*   Yes, considering the kids hadn't done anything to them. Well,

they might have done something to them before that, but you don't know that ... they generally just pick on them anyway, don't they?

(*Later*)

41 *Seb:* I mean, some blacks are all right, because there was a cancer research thing up at the Arts and Crafts market the other week the paper and they were charging us and there was only one shop in the whole of this area that said they'd pay the kids to do it and that was the black people in the newsagents up Lawn Wood. They were the only ones that said they'd pay.

42 *Alan:* Pay what?

43 *Seb:* Pay the paper lads to deliver extra, instead of us having to give them money to do it.

44 *Alan:* Yeah.

45 *Seb:* So some of them are all right.

This is not exactly the most enlightened example of an open-minded discussion of race. Indeed it is shot through with examples of shameful ignorance and prejudice on the part of all three boys. Even in their least bigoted moments there is an air of disdainful patronisation in the ideas expressed. But let us not expect too much. In the whole-class discussion the boys had solidly backed the 'racist' point of view against the part of the teacher. Nowhere was there a chink in their armour. When we look carefully at these transcripts there are some glimmers of light.

Ignoring for the moment the layers of prejudice they are embedded in, the following comments may well indicate some very small steps for mankind, but some giant leaps from these boys. In (2) Alan surprisingly expresses the enlightened view of the enriching nature of cultural mixes, immediately shared by Seb, but countered by Mick. Seb (whose views seem to be in his words '50/50') denies in his own way the racist views heard in the whole class discussion that blacks are 'taking over the country' by explaining that the multi-ethnic population is concentrated in certain areas. What he actually says is 'they hang around in the Midlands' which does not sound too complimentary to us nicely-brought-up, middle-class teachers, but let us not put *our* moral grids over *their* language. Seb simply does not *know* the 'acceptable' terms. Alan continues in (7) to counter the earlier expressed 'send-'em-home' views by explaining that ethnic minorities are no longer immigrants but British citizens. There are a number of very patronising references to black people known to be 'all right' (from Mick in (9) and Seb in (10) and (41)). I squirm whenever I hear this particular line of thought, but the point here is that I am convinced that the boys would never have put forward these alternative angles in the whole-class discussion. The smaller group is a more private, honest arena.

There is an interesting discussion phase between (14–19). Here Mick begins by criticising racial abuse. Seb throws the arguments back at him by saying that 'they call us honkies, don't they?' The 'don't they?' is a positive invitation to wheel out the peer-group street norms. Instead, Mick in these more intimate circumstances counters Seb coolly and objectively by saying in (19), 'I've never heard a black kid call anybody a honky'.

The discussion continues at an anecdotal level and Mick tells a story that has obviously been an important influence in shaping his views. There must be more to this particular story, but it comes across as an honestly expressed one (again, would he tell this so readily to a mixed class of 25 peers?). Mick responds in (29) and (35) by explaining to the embittered Seb in his own language that this is an unfortunate response to the treatment they have received.

This may well get through to Mick and Alan who go on in (37) and (38) to express their disapproval of overt and publicly-expressed racist activity. Mick confirms their line of thought when he tells another story from personal experience where he witnessed racial harassment. The crucial factor here is that he overlays it with his own feelings: 'I feel sorry for them', something he would have found inappropriate in the whole class.

Seb's story of the Asian shopkeeper in (41) continues in this line of exploring their own experience for examples which go against current street norms. We can perhaps shelve the comment 'some blacks are all right' which prefaces his story. That is his 'way in', whereas we middle-class teachers would have searched for a more appropriate introduction. The story is no less strongly felt for its unfortunate beginning.

My feeling is that these boys are here opening up the armour of peer-group norms which enclosed them in the whole-class discussions, to let some objective thought shine through and to allow for the exploration of experiences and *feelings* which could only be expressed in this secure smaller group of trusted peers.

Peter, the most obviously vocal and mindlessly racist member of the group, was absent during the above discussion. The next day he appeared back in the class and I asked him if he would talk for a few minutes with me, outside the class, about the earlier discussion. I asked him directly whether he liked or disliked black people. After a pause for thought of five seconds, he said: 'Well, I like some and I don't like some. I had some black mates at the other school. They were all right ... but some of them cause trouble and stuff like some whites do.'

The familiar 'the-ones-I-know-are-OK' syndrome is here complemented by the curiously enlightened and unexpected response that some whites cause trouble. Why would he add that? Could it be that he is, in this private discussion, being Peter the ordinary human being, rather than adopting his public image of 'Peter the racist: good for a laugh'? He goes on to say: 'Sometimes I say things to rile the teacher up ... Mr X he likes all kinds of races ... not a fascist or anything ... he's one of those Left-wing trendies ... I wind him up about all these blacks and stuff.'

In a later discussion with a group of girls, they commented that they enjoyed talking with others as it was a 'mind-broadening' experience. I raised the problem of Peter:

Me: You talk about broadening the mind, well wouldn't that *narrow* the mind if you kept hearing that sort of stuff?
Sally: Yes it would.
Samantha: He's like that all the time ... his dad's laden with it, you see, so anyone who's not got as much as he has, they're peasants.
Sally: You get used to Peter but you just think he's stupid.
Samantha: If it was somebody you didn't know, something like that would ...
Sally: Yes, 'praps but we know what Peter's like ... we know he's only mucking around.
Samantha: But he (*indistinct*) ... can't think. He makes stupid comments because he hasn't got anything sensible to say.

Like the girls in my class quoted earlier, these girls do not share the racist's view of things; equally they do not see the whole-class arena as the place to challenge peer-group norms.

I have made the case earlier for talk being a means of exploring new ideas, broadening the mental horizons. It appears from these several tapes that this purpose is best fulfilled within the context of purposeful, committed smaller-group work, where young people can be more honest and directly personal, where it is inappropriate to conform to blinkering self-images and street norms and where the moral flavour of the talk is directed by the peer group itself rather than by instinctive responses to adult control.

In an earlier chapter I tried to point out how whole-class discussions can simply become a game of guessing what teacher wants you to say. The above analysis offers the view that larger groups can inhibit the kind of personal and open responses that lead to moments of learning and development.

Is the whole class therefore an inappropriate arena for *any* kind of talk for learning? Are the problems associated with it inevitable? Before we dismiss it, let us review its weaknesses and explore solutions.

Problems with whole-class discussion

Four problems can be isolated. First, the teacher is the dominant figure and can manipulate discussion so that it becomes a meaningless game. Comments are channelled through the teacher-as-loudspeaker, so discussion does not flow naturally. The following extract from a discussion with ten-year-olds about dogs fouling pavements illustrates this:

Teacher: Any other ideas?
Pupil: You could have holes in the gutter and they could train dogs to do it in there.

Teacher: Holes in the gutter, that's a good idea ... what do people think about that? Yes?
Pupil: But some old people need their dogs as companions.
Teacher: Ah! But we're talking about dog mess on the pavements at the moment. Yes, Sean?
Pupil: I think they should keep them out of parks.

This is a series of isolated statements on a theme rather than a mutual exploration of ideas.

Second, the discussion is dominated by a few confident pupils. I would not need to do a piece of quantitative research to be able to demonstrate that less talking by students is done in whole-class discussions. The amount of talk increases in direct proportion to the number of groups. Let us say, in an average-sized class of 28 split into groups of four or five, there is a six-fold increase in work output. Many more people speak. Pupils like Anne and Sue get a chance.

Third, the discussion is not sufficiently open, personal or exploratory. The public, large-group situation does not encourage some children, especially boys, to express and explore their more subtle thoughts and feelings. They are talking to a varied collection of individuals with whom it is difficult to take risks.

Fourth, the participants cannot hear clearly what is said without lots of hushing and 'can-you-speak-ups' by the teacher-as-loudspeaker/ringmaster.

These four problems share three basic, related factors: the teacher's awareness of the learning process; the physical context of the classroom; and the emotional context of the classroom.

First, teacher awareness. If a teacher knows what he or she is trying to enable to happen in a class discussion and can recognise fruitful learning-talk then he or she will be sensitive to what is happening in general and to his or her own contribution in particular. This is a matter of awareness, born of understanding and experience. Underpinning this is a necessary commitment to a process-based learning model which will put the emphasis on the pupils themselves talking in a more open way.

Second, the physical context. It is very difficult, if not impossible, actually to have a shared discussion with upwards of 25 pupils dotted around a classroom. As I have tried to show, there is a deference to the teacher's domination of procedure and thought, and a natural tendency to lapse into a series of isolated statements channelled through the teacher-as-loudspeaker.

To break this mould you will need to move the furniture so that everyone can hear everybody else speak and so the teacher can become part of the discussion rather than the dominant chairperson. A rule of thumb should be that anyone involved in the discussion should be able to take one step forward and punch anyone else on the nose without over-stretching. That way the discussion is more immediately personal. Pupils begin to talk directly to each other, to individuals rather than to the whole class (via the teacher). As far as possible pupils will need to be facing each other.

The discussion recorded towards the end of this chapter took place in a class of 25 13-year-olds. Used to sitting in grouped clusters of desks, they had been asked twice before to move the furniture so that there was an outer horseshoe (or circle if you wish) of desks on which 14 of them sat and an inner circle of chairs on which 11 sat. The teacher sat on a chair in the 'gap' of the horseshoe. This arrangement entailed the minimum of movement but with a little more rearrangement could have been made into a circle. The teacher could then take her place *amongst* the pupils. The time required to set up this situation was never more than two minutes once the pupils were used to it. I would estimate that at least two minutes are lost in any whole-classroom discussion by the teacher repeating comments some people cannot hear.

Third, the emotional context. Even if the physical context is right pupils will not wish to venture into personal, tentative talk if the atmosphere of the classroom is not right. I have already examined two examples where pupils have been inhibited in whole-class discussion and have either expressed stereotyped views they do not really hold, or simply kept quiet and not revealed their true opinions about what was said. I suspect that the attitude of the teacher, the kind of classroom he or she is trying to run, is crucial in all this, and difficult to alter if things are not going well. All will depend on the answer to these sorts of question. Do you actually like your pupils and value what they say? Can your classroom be run smoothly and in an orderly way, whilst you remain essentially a warm and pleasant human being? What kind of learning experiences are you trying to make happen, anyway?

The teacher's answers to these questions can subtly affect the 'chemistry' of the classroom, the collective attitude of the pupils to each other and to the learning process. A powerful and intractable clique to whom the rest of the class defer can be an impossible barrier, as can the solo individual, the professional discussion-wrecker that Peter (above) proved to be. I am forcefully reminded of his devastating contribution to a film on the production of bananas where he conducted a kind of running commentary. Here are some extracts:

> Hey ... look at big mama ... BIG MARMA ... look at the eyes on her ... you see them banana boats ... that's how all them blackies get here ... painting themselves yellow and hiding in a crate of nanas ... £2 a day ... what are they moaning about ... they're only a bunch of blackie skivvies.

No wonder that the subsequent discussion fell flat on its face.

If teachers really value open and exploratory discussion they must be prepared to be very clear about their expectations and make them understood by the class. Discussion-wreckers need to be dealt with firmly and decisively. This should not cut across the need for a warm and caring atmosphere. Such an atmosphere will simply not exist, laced by comments such as Peter's. The other pupils would not resent his rights to be in the classroom being suspended. What would be our response if someone persistently scribbled all over the writing individuals (or the whole class) were involved in, or wrecked other people's craftwork? If we value talk equally with other modes of learning then we must be prepared to work hard to nurture the right atmosphere and treat individuals who try to spoil it with consistent firmness.

So if the above conditions are met and we have a teacher with the necessary sensitivity to talk as a learning process, and both the physical and the emotional contexts are as right as they can be, can productive learning-talk take place amongst 25 teenagers gathered together in one place?

Let us have a look at another extract. This is a discussion with a third-year secondary English group on the subject of sexism. There had been an important prelude to the discussion. Small mixed groups had discussed a list of statements on the topic to see what they felt about them. In the whole group they were asked to highlight and introduce the statements they felt strongly about either way. In this extract they are talking about the suggestion that girls need stricter 'coming-in' times than boys.

> Sean: If the girl's out ... there's all sort of men that says something like 'Hello, love' and chat them up to get them in the car, or something, then probably kill them or something ... They're not going to do it much often to a boy, are they? ... boys usually hang about in bigger gangs ... say a man tries to harass a girl or boy, the boy's gonna stand more of a chance, isn't he, at the age of 14?
>
> Katie: I think that more lads get into trouble with the police than girls do ... so if the girls are out later, they don't have to (*indistinct*) so much as lads do and then they don't get into trouble ... I mean girls don't start throwing bricks and things like that.
>
> Sean: Yes ... but neither do all the boys.
>
> Katie: Not *all* boys do.
>
> Sean: Not all the boys go round throwing bricks, do they?
>
> Katie: Not all the boys do, but a lot of boys get into trouble.
>
> Esmee: I mean, if you're hanging round the street and you're in a disco, then what's the difference what time you go home as long as you've got a lift and you're sensible ... and if you're outside in the streets ... you should both come in early, shouldn't you? If you're in the streets then you both shouldn't stay out late 'cos boys can get into trouble and girls can get hurt.
>
> John: You say that when you go to discos, you're all right as long as you're sensible and you've got a lift home, but ... lads ... some people when they get with their mates ... they just start acting dead stupid.

We would need to have videoed this to get the full flavour. As it is you must take it from me that, despite the disagreements, the talk has a thoughtful, non-aggressive tone. But above all, the pupils are talking directly to each other, across the horseshoe of listeners, rather than making isolated statements through the teacher/ringmaster. The teacher simply sat through this sharing the discussion with the others. In this way a genuine dialogue is set up and Katie feels able to take on the arguments advanced by Sean (a powerful figure in the class). The two explore some common ground and get further than Sean's opening generalisation. Esmee then adds a new dimension to the discussion. Her non-assertive, questioning tone is a result of her talking directly with interested peers in a controlled situation. John is able then to keep the conversation flowing by picking up one of her points and showing it in a new light. There is movement of thought here rather than bald polarisation of ideas. It is a more collective response to the topic.

In the next extract the discussion has moved on to dress:

James: Pink hair looks worse on a girl than it does on a boy. (*Babble of responses*)

Ian: Why would pink hair look better on a boy?

James: I dunno.

Dianne: Pink's more trendy for boys to wear now.

James: It depends what you're wearing. If it's pink shoes, it does look a bit ... puffy ... but if you're wearing a pink shirt.

Ian: If you had your hair dyed all pink though, if you came to school, everyone would laugh at you even if they *did* like it.

James: Everyone laughs at everyone when he's had his hair short ... but after about a week later they don't think nothing of it ... probably kids that ain't seen him they'd say 'God ... look at him ... doesn't he look a state?' or something, but after they'd got used to seeing him it's all right.

David: What about the blokes in films. They have to wear make-up, don't they?

Anne: Nobody in here's got dyed hair, really ... no boys that is.

James: I had my ear pierced.

Anne: But you've not got it now, have you?

James: But if I did it doesn't mean I'm a puff, does it?

Teacher: Can I just interrupt a minute? Can I just ask about make-up. What do you feel about that?

Ian: Oh yes! Boys. Boys don't go about wearing lipstick.

John: And why not? Why not?

Ian: Because it would look pathetic, wouldn't it?

Dianne: They can wear make-up if they want to, but I wouldn't go out with a lad who wears make-up.

Teacher: You *wouldn't* want to? Can you tell me why?

Dianne: Dunno ... I'd think he was queer going around with a girl.

Jenny: All make-up looks OK if you use it to make yourself more attractive, so if a boy wants to wear make-up to make himself more attractive ... (*indistinct*) ... it's not all stupid or anything.

James: Yeah ... I agree with that.

Ian: I don't.

This extract has the flavour and texture of a small-group discussion, despite the fact that it is the record of the contribution of half-a-dozen pupils within a group of 25. Again, they talk directly to each other. Note the questions asked by Ian ('Why would pink hair look better on a boy?') and John ('And why not? Why not?'). The questions show they are listening and involved in the discussion and show a very healthy desire to challenge assertions, not by making a polarised counter-statement, but by throwing the ball back in the court of the speaker. That kind of immediate and natural response is difficult to generate in a spread-out class of pupils putting their hands up to await their turn to speak. It is the sort of response that one would normally associate with the teacher/chairperson. How much more powerful and effective that the challenging questions should be asked directly by the pupils. Indeed it is interesting to examine the role of the teacher here. At one point she asks permission to *interrupt* the flow – clear evidence of how she sees her role as an enabler, a participant rather than a dominant figure. Note how both her interventions do not decisively shift the ground of the discussion, but seek to probe in a helpful way, to move the discussion along by asking the genuinely *open* questions: 'What do you feel about that?' and 'Can you tell me why?'.

Compare this style with the 'search for silt' in Chapter 5 where questions were used to elicit the 'right' response. The situation set up above by the teacher has enabled these self-conscious 13-year-olds to explore important issues in a thoughtful way, as equals in the journey to understanding. They clearly have a long way to go yet (the consensus about 'puffs' needs examination) but there is a partnership, a desire to collaborate in the consideration of the issues, to worry at them together which gives me hope.

I believe nevertheless that the staple diet of classroom talk should take place within smaller groups of trusted peers. It is important, too, that ideas are shared and explored in larger groups because it is vital that classroom talk takes place in a rich variety of contexts, where there are subtly different pressures and expectations. I would like to feel that young people were not too overawed by the larger groupings of people who very often determine the everyday fate of other people. The examples I have quoted throughout this book show how much young people could contribute to public debate.

8 The nature of the task

There are, I believe, two main variables affecting the success of learning-talk. The first, discussed in the previous chapter, is the context of the talk in terms of the environment and pupil groupings: the arena where the talk takes place. In this chapter I am concerned to explore the second variable; what teachers actually ask pupils to do when they talk together.

Ten years after Bullock we are just beginning to get clues about this. Many of us learned the hard way that you cannot simply ask groups of children to discuss something and hope that they will get going. Though no amount of thought and preparation will ever legislate for success in talk, I am convinced that we can now begin to draw up guidelines for talk which minimise the chance of spectacular failure. Let me reduce these guidelines to a simplistic few for the purposes of discussion: the task should be of interest to the pupils; the task should be an open one, where a number of responses ('answers' if you like) are possible; and there should be as far as possible a purposeful and understood 'outcome' from the talk.

'It's got to be interesting'

As part of the earlier-quoted investigation of pupil attitudes to talk as a means of learning, we interviewed a number of pupils to try to find out their ideas about making talk lessons go more successfully. One plea that cropped up consistently was that, whatever was being talked about and in whatever context, it must be interesting. 'It's got to be interesting' ... 'if they're interested they'll talk about it more' ... 'you'll probably do more work and everybody will be more enthusiastic'. 'If they say "Do you want a whole-group discussion on school uniform or a small-group discussion on something else?", I'd choose the large group.' So people talk more if they are interested in something. If this appears a rather obvious point it begs a number of questions.

What actually makes us, you and I, interested in something? I suspect that the answer is closely tied up with the other variables mentioned above, but of one thing I am sure; we cannot *expect* pupils to be interested *per se* in *anything*, however carefully we pick the topic. Young people have all sorts of things on their minds. Our aim must be to bring whatever is discussed to the front of their minds, the very tips of their tongues. We can do this perhaps by asking them what they want to talk about, and allowing them to choose the area for discussion and to thereby set the agenda for learning. This may be possible in the primary classroom or in a number of humanities-related subjects where the main focus is on the means; we want them simply to discuss and the subject is less important than the rehearsal of the process of discussion itself. So I have witnessed some excellent discussion sessions in English, focusing on pupils trying to sort out what the function could be of a strange unknown object, or devising as many uses as possible for an ordinary household brick.

In other areas we may wish the pupils to come to a greater understanding of particular ideas, concepts or texts through talking with others. If the essential spark of interest is not there, we must work hard to create it. It may be that we will need to set up preliminary fore-play before the act of discussion can begin in earnest and with enthusiasm. In the past I have used film, pictures, role-play, tape or text to do this. Somehow we must aim to engender that necessary spark before the discussion can catch fire. I have seen so many discussions, whether in small or large groups, founder because this 'rule' has been broken.

Keep it open

Pupils need to feel they have a stake in what is going on, that they have a valid contribution to make and that their ideas can add to the collective store of knowledge within the class or group. They cannot feel this if the aim of the talk seems to be to come to some conclusion for which there is a right or wrong answer lurking behind the set task. We can't expect pupils to take risks, be open, personal, exploratory or tentative when to do so might invite failure. The greatest single cause of reticence amongst pupils is fear of making a fool of themselves – that is, giving a wrong or silly answer. So to ask pupils 'to list the seven major causes of pollution' is less likely to generate successful learning than the following more concrete and specific questions:

1 Describe examples of pollution you come across in the areas where you live.
2 Using ideas above, try to make some general points about the major causes of pollution in this area.

This is more than a matter of mere semantics. There is, too, an implied shift in the teaching/learning model.

A NASA test, widely used in schools, gives a list of items which someone stranded on the moon has available – but he/she can only use a certain number. There is an exact right answer to the test, which was used as a kind of intelligence test for identifying potential astronauts. If we gave the task to pupils with these sorts of parameters I suspect they would not respond so well to it as they would if given the same list and told 'there is no right answer to this. Sort out your own ideas and compare them with someone else's. Try to come to an agreed list of five items which you feel are essential.'

From this it will be clear that a major influence on the nature and success of a discussion session, whether in the whole class or a small group, is the nature of the questions asked by the teacher. Implied in this is the question of the teacher's stance towards the learners and the learning process.

A purposeful and understood outcome

Not all educational activity requires a product by which the learning can be judged. So often it is the work, thought and talk leading up to the product which is the valuable part. Pupils could in fact throw away much of the 'stuff' they finally produce and not be any less educated as a result. However, it may be necessary to have a product to work towards, a perceived purposeful outcome for the talk, if the talk is to be successful. Talk needs to be about something and needs to be moving somewhere (if your classes are anything like mine). So it is not enough, for example, to ask a group to 'talk about pollution' – which could lead to some drifting and desultory chat; if, however, you ask the group to sort a number of statements, pre-prepared on strips of paper, into those they agree with or those they disagree with, the talk has more chance of both being focused and flowing. Even better if you ask them to prepare their own versions of such statements for others to work with.

Asking pupils to answer questions on a poem together (however open they may be and however good the poem) is less likely to succeed than to ask them to prepare six questions to ask about the poem for another group to consider. In the one model you are trying to get them to understand the poem through your questions, in the other model they are in an active situation, generating their own questions for a particular audience. On the journey they must of necessity have considered the poem carefully.

In Chapter 5 I described how pupils working separately on similar tasks tend to chat all the time about non-task-related, relatively trivial topics. If you shift the emphasis of the task so that they are working together on the same task, the talk will flow without your prompting and without the need for carefully prepared lists of questions. Remaining with the pollution topic, we might, for example, ask pupils in groups of three or four to produce montages or collages on the theme of pollution, consisting of real-life examples, quotes from textbooks, pictures, statistics, snippets of poetry – again, concrete and specific suggestions.

We would not in these circumstances be saying 'talk about pollution' but we would be setting up situations which call forth language, in which the pupils have to talk to proceed, and where the talk is focused on the classroom agenda. I have consistently found that practical tasks of doing and making centring on real objects are far more likely to generate learning-talk successfully than the more academic, dry, unnatural tasks of answering abstract questions.

An example

I wish now to describe a particular example of a task which fulfilled the criteria above and which led to several lessons of fruitful learning-talk. What is particularly interesting about this example is that it comes from a sequence of work, described in Chapter 5, where one of the opening sessions was the closed discussion about silt. The subject the third-year Humanities class was focusing on was natural disasters. The initial whole-class discussion was designed to get ideas flowing, and to give a background of facts for the next stage. The pupils were asked in groups to work towards a presentation of a 10 o'clock news item which told viewers of a natural disaster which had just happened. The pupils were asked to include factual information about the disaster, a general introduction about its cause, illustrative material, diagrams and interviews.

Within minutes of the task being set up the room was buzzing with talk – that busy, involved, concentrated talk that you can just feel is right. They had not been *asked* to talk, but the situation demanded that they did so, with a real purpose and with the determination and concentration generated by a given deadline: they had three one-hour lessons before they had to present. The deadline, far from being a limiting factor, was in my view a creative release. They knew they had a certain time-span and tailored their work accordingly. The work rate in these circumstances was very high. Neither of the two teachers nor I came across any pupils wasting time or messing about during this phase of work. That was extraordinary, given the general reputation in schools of third-year classes. We were constantly in demand and bombarded with 'real' questions. Released from the pressure of being 'up front' we took on the role of advisers and enablers. The groups barely noticed the tape recorders lying here and there, so involved were they with the task. Here is a short slice from a tape of a group of boys at work.

Neil: Right . . . I'm going to do the news write-up now.
Chris: What will you say on that?
Neil: Like . . . um . . . saying that it was caused by . . . um . . . what shall I say it was caused by?

Chris: I dunno anything about 'em.
Neil: It comes out from the winds, doesn't it?
Chris: Just say it started in the Indian Ocean and it worked its way
            toward Mozambique.
Neil: Shall we ask Miss M ... ?
            (*Two minutes later*)
Teacher: Do you want some help?
Neil: How are cyclones caused by ... ?
Teacher: What are they caused by ... ? Differences in temperature and the
            movement of air between different places ... if I get you the book,
            I think the book will explain it ... or I can explain it with the
            book.
Neil: OK.
            (*Another group called a teacher over to check on their work.*)
Boy 1:   Mr M ... You know the paths of these cyclones? ...
Teacher: Yes.
Boy 1:   Is there anywhere we can find the paths?
Teacher: The path of a cyclone?
Boy 1:   Yes, because I've got ones from South America or North America.
Teacher: I can't show you one in a map, but I can just show you what is a
            likely path. Why can't you have it originating here in the Indian
            Ocean ... and then moving on ...
Boy 2:   Yes.
Teacher: And then moving in a circular pattern in towards, let's say, the
            Bay of Bengal.
Boy 2:   That's where we've done it in the Bay of Bengal.
Teacher: Fine ... so what are you asking me?
Boy 2:   Well, would it start up there?
Teacher: Well, it would start in the Indian Ocean because that's where you
            get the differentials in pressure.
Boy 1:   Ah yes.
Boy 2:   That's why there's so many ... (*indistinct*) round the Equator,
            isn't it? ... Because of the differences in pressure ...
Teacher: Yes ... the temperature differences produce differences of air
            pressure ...

The task has generated the need to know amongst these pupils. In these circumstances they can learn quickly and accept the expertise of the book and the short-cuts offered by asking real questions of the teacher – and by that I mean questions that they are genuinely curious to find the answer to. The final comment of Boy 2 above shows that this is not just the gathering of soon-to-be-forgotten information but the acquiring of knowledge which can be related or fitted in to what he already knows. In another example (overheard, not taped) a boy asked the teacher to explain high and low pressure winds. The teacher did so by using the illustration of a bicycle tyre being let down. In their later presentation the boys used precisely this analogy and showed a fluent grasp of the concept.

Learning, in these circumstances, sticks. I later talked to this lad and asked him why he chose to call over the teacher to solve his difficulty rather than refer to one of the many reference books available. 'I'd rather talk to the teacher than read it in a book,' he replied. 'The book doesn't explain it well ... if you don't understand something he [the teacher] can explain it ... If you don't understand about the book you can't ask it ... you can always ask the teacher again.'

Written material is too impersonal and one-way a source of information for this particular pupil. Books were very heavily in use, however, throughout the classroom. Indexes were scanned and pages flicked through during the determined and purposeful finding-out.

Because the news item was to be presented and rehearsed, many of the groups were busy creating text jointly:

Girl 1: (*Reading*) 'Although Wales is probably the worst affected one, it's by no means the worst and' ...

Girl 2: Ah! No: 'in Wales' ... you say 'most affected area in Wales'. Otherwise it sounds a bit stupid.

Girl 1: 'Although Wales was probably the worst affected area ... it was by no means the worst ...'

Girl 2: Hang on! You can't do that ... you can't ...

Girl 3: You've just said that it was the worst, but it's not the worst ... there were other affected areas.

Girl 1: 'Although Wales was probably the worst affected area ... it was by no means ...'

Girl 2: The only one.

Girl 1: (*Writing*) 'the only one'.

Here by reading aloud and by careful listening to the text, the girls edit it jointly, ironing out anomalies, alert for problems of sense and register.

In the next example a group of girls are fastidiously and purposefully worrying away at their text to get the exact register and format of the news item. They work entirely collaboratively and a kind of shared thinking aloud is in evidence throughout. They sound out the words, test the stylistic conventions. They are co-operating over the production of a subtle and complex piece of language. Strong comments are made but no one seems to resent the suggestions about reworking. The task in hand must be right and nothing is taken personally. The deadline has created a single-minded discipline in the group. This extract is from a 20-minute tape of them intensely at work.

Girl 1: (*Reading*) 'Good evening ... we have a report on the terrible catastrophe in Sudan ... and now over to Katie Monk in Sudan.'

Girl 2: (*Reading*) 'Two and a half million people are starving in Sudan. The situation is now as bad as Ethiopia. They haven't had any rain for several years and I am going to ask the Red Cross worker now how the famine came. Excuse me, can you tell me what happened?'

Girl 4: 'Yes ... we need, lots of rain but there is none ... When there is no ...'

Girl 3: That's not what happened.

Girl 2: Shut up Louise.

Girl 4: 'Animals grow thin and die. People have nothing to eat and die as well ...'

Girl 2: We've got it completely ... let's change that ... Let's change that.

Girl 3: That's a bit stupid there.

Girl 2: Let's get my pen for a minute ... Right then ... put 'Good evening' at the beginning ... right like that ... put 'Good evening' and put 'Alison' so that we know who's saying it ... right ... er ... we could have.

Girl 3: No we're starting again.

Girl 4: Because it's too short.

Girl 3: 'We have a report ... tonight ...'

Girl 2: Right ... 'We have a report' ... Don't put about the terrible catastrophe ... coming from Sudan ... say ... 'We have a report on' ... er ... no ... 'We have a report coming from ... um ... Sudan'.

Girl 3: No 'We have a report ... live ...'

Girl 2: 'from Sudan ...'. Yeah.

Girl 3: (*Writing*) We ... have ... a ...

Girl 2: 'Report ... live ... from ... Sudan' ... er ... 'live ... from ... Sudan' ... right ... 'live from Sudan ... so we go over to ... er ...'

Girl 3: No, we can't just put that!

Girl 2: Yeah! 'Live from Sudan ...' about the disaster ... no, about the drought.

Girl 3: No ... we'll have to start a new sentence ... say 'Good evening. Tonight we have a report live from Sudan ...'

Girl 2: 'Sudan' ... yes ... 'About the terrible tragedy that is happening ...'. No ... you don't have to say that.

Girl 3: Don't put anything.

Girl 1: I know ... we can change the actual report ...

Girl 2: You didn't really say about the ...

Girl 1: You wouldn't just go 'Good evening. We have a report on the terrible catastrophe in Sudan ... and now we go over to Katie Monk'.

Girl 3: It's not right ... is it? You'd have a very serious voice ...

The following week two whole lessons were taken up by the presentations. All the groups had managed to meet the deadlines, some in a better state of preparation than others. One group had made a home video, another had produced their item entirely through animated computer-presentation. Most had used a mixture of tape, diagram and text to give a succinct account and explanation of the disaster they had chosen. One group had ingeniously invented a hitherto unknown cause for a disaster. It was this which confirmed my impression that the real educational value of this sequence was not to do with the learning and understanding of content, though undoubtedly the class knew more about the topic at the end of the sequence than they did at the outset.

No, what they were learning which will last them longer than bits of information was the hidden agenda of the sequence. These 13-year-olds were learning to work together on a common, purposeful task; to agree objectives; to share responsibilities; to pay careful attention to the language and register of text; to present something clearly so that someone else can understand; to refine and adapt materials until they are as right as they can be. Would an employer value these qualities and experiences rather more than knowledge about how natural disasters originate? I suspect so. The medium through which all this 'real learning' took place was talk. For five lessons the room was swimming in talk. The slot in the timetable said 'Humanities'. Like all successful sequences of work the learning transcended the label on the classroom door.

9 The learning model

If I tell you, you will forget. If I show you, you will remember.
If I involve you, you will understand.

Police Sergeant, Henley Training Centre

Chapter 6, in its consideration of barriers to the use of talk in schools, briefly offered the view that a content-based model of teaching and learning, with its accompanying emphasis on teacher control and the transmission of information, tends to squeeze out talk as a central means of learning. I would like to explore further the implication of that notion.

Content-based teaching says: 'This is reality; my job is to induct you into it in as painless a way as possible.' In this model, reality is non-negotiable, a fixed entity external to the learner. Watts (1980, p. 57) points out a few cracks in this model: 'The teacher can no longer safely predict what information needs to be known in any subject in order to equip his students for life after school'. He goes on to propose a more appropriate teacher role for a complex and rapidly-changing world.

> The teacher is above all person-centred, more concerned with the student as he or she is, than as something to be formed ... We do not know what will become of our students or of our children; we don't even know what they need to know; we can only assist them as they are (p. 89).

Watts is implying here a process-based model of learning, or, as Barnes (1976) puts it, an 'interpretative' model as opposed to a 'transmission' model. Barnes says:

> The more a teacher sees knowledge as a valued possession associated with his present status and future aspirations, the less of a part one might expect him to accord to his pupils in shaping the knowledge which is given public recognition in his lesson (p. 151).

If the teacher is, then, to shift to this more appropriate interpretative model of education, where talk moves to the centre of activities, the leap must be made to the premise that each new learner embraces a reality and shapes it to fit his or her own meanings, the emerging picture in his or her head. In this model of learning reality is, in essence, negotiable.

To make room for such a process-based model, teachers must ditch the lesson structures that they have so lovingly developed over the years and that have ensured their survival. This will be a painful process. They must in a sense turn their back on years of what seemed to them to be good-enough practice; they must cast out all the old furniture and begin planning again in another house. In these new plans they can maintain a leadership role but they are no longer the source of wisdom, the ringmaster. The learners are now actively involved in the planning and carrying through of classroom acts. What they bring to the classroom is more important than what the teacher brings. They are now, in a very real sense, the *experts* and the teacher is the setter-up, the enabler, the prompter, encourager, the monitor and the assessor.

How might all this look in the classroom? I want to analyse below a particular sequence of work with ten-year-olds that tried to put into practice the above ideas, tried to offer a new learning model where the pupil was at the centre, and where talk was the means of negotiating reality.

Having our say

During my year as an action-researcher in one family of schools, I spent time in a final-year junior classroom studying how these ten-year-olds were using talk to learn, with a view to identifying areas that the teacher and I could try to develop. Following a period of informal observation, we decided to set up a situation where children were encouraged to explore their views about particular issues important to them. We wanted them to take the opportunity to talk these issues through with other people in an extended way and in the context of a purposeful task. In these circum-stances, previous instincts may have led us to set up something for everyone to do on a topic such as fox-hunting. But there were two of us and so we were prepared to take a few risks.

So began 'Campaign'. After an introduction by us of a 'model', the children were asked to jot down the things they felt strongly about to introduce to others on their table. Ideas at this stage ranged from the intensely personal and local (softer toilet paper for the girls' loos) to the wide, global sweep (food for all). Some were then publicly aired and everyone was asked to join with a group of two or three others to work on the same 'cause'. We had anticipated this as a sticky moment. In the event there was a lot of negotiation, moving about, claiming of friends, changing of opinions, for a period of about ten minutes before groups miraculously settled down together. One group was too large, one changed its mem-bership several times and one boy could not get anyone to support his cause – he carried on nevertheless.

We wanted them now to focus their thoughts and to devise a coherent, purposeful way of working. Each group was asked to work together on an agreed campaign aims statement and a snappy title. So emerged the campaigns to change the meals system to a cafeteria, to stop canal pollution, save trees, allow ten-year-olds to vote, destroy all bombs, set up more youth activities in their area and to stop animals being used in experiments. Once these had been vetted by us then the groups immediately got going on a list of possible things to do in their campaign: petitions, letters, interviews, posters ... and badges. The latter was an afterthought from the teacher who was looking for a creative use for a supply of tacky-back covering paper he had acquired. From these the children could very quickly mass-produce stick-on labels with their campaign logo. This turned out to have the inspiring simplicity of all good teaching/learning ideas. The children wanted to persuade others to wear their badges. To do this they had to argue the cause and we issued the general advice to everyone: 'Don't wear badges if you're not convinced.' Very soon the classroom was absolutely humming with committed private discussions, disputes, conversations, harangues, as the children tried to give away their badges. The premium was to get an adult wearing one. We did not give our favours lightly. At dinnertime the work spilled out from the classroom. Playground supervisors, and caretakers, were besieged by campaigning children clutching badges and petitions. It was this early phase that generated the most sustained, intense and purposeful discussion of issues that we have witnessed amongst final-year juniors. Their stamina was amazing as they approached person after person. They learned to reply to points made against them and counter-arguments were developed and refined until the campaigners became seasoned veterans. We had not quite anticipated this. In many ways our aims would have been achieved if the group had simply spent a morning on this phase. The badges were the key to it all.

When the groups were trying to persuade us to wear their badges or sign their petitions we tape-recorded their discussions. Here is an example of what went on, in an extract from a discussion with three boys about stopping animal experiments.

Teacher: Right, can you explain to me why I should sign that petition?
Paul: Well, it's obvious that we want to get more people so we can stop
...
Robert: Yeah, so we can prove to the people who are higher up, who've got some chance of doing something, that it's a good thing to do.
Teacher: Right ... before I sign it, you've got to prove to me that it's a good thing to do, then.
Robert: Well, we've got our statement (*reads*): 'Our aim is to cut out cruelty to animals, also to stop scientists testing drugs on animals and also testing new weapons on them. Please sign below if you agree with us. We will send this petition to the *Leicester Mercury*.'
Teacher: OK ... now how can you prove to me that animals suffer?
Robert: Well, we've got some sort of ideas because my mum, she did, when she was teaching she did a project on it and she's got a book

and it's got ... we really just think the animals are suffering because of the way they're doing it ...

Ben: For no reason ...

Robert: If the animals have not got a chance to speak for themselves, if they were above us, and we were going to be ... they were testing to try and find cures for rabies and they were doing something nasty to us, and we didn't know about it, because we couldn't talk, it wouldn't ...

Paul: Every time they do a new test out, they kill an animal – it's just like killing a human.

Robert: Yes, because I read a bit of this page and it said this doctor he cut an eye ... er he cut ... um ... optic nerve in one of the cat's eyes, and then a few weeks later he cut the optic nerve and killed the cat.

Teacher: But what if that helps a human being to see; say he's doing research into blindness or something, and by making that cat blind ...

Robert: We don't ... He's *killing* the cat at the end (*Paul*: Yeah). He's killing it when it's got no eyesight left, instead of just let ... of having the cat just blind. He takes both the eyes out so he can study 'em.

         Later (about testing weapons on animals)

Teacher: You think that's wrong do you?

Paul: Yes, because they're just testing on an animal to kill other people.

All three: Sometimes when they have it, they have model kind of men ... that's on models ... and model animals, and they fire at that ... and they try it on moving targets ... yeah, and they're just as good ... but they don't use animals at it ... we'd rather them do it on models instead of ... they test animals to see if when it hits them it will actually kill the animal.

Ben: Yes ... they test the things, they don't need to make (animals suffer? – *indistinct*) at all.

Robert: Just to find out if a man would die if you did it to him.

There are several interesting features here, beyond the fact that this was a good example of an extended, intense exchange of ideas (the whole tape lasts for seven minutes).

The struggle for language is there as the children work at the limits of their linguistic consciousness (witness the straining for 'the optic nerve'), but it is eased by the pressure of sheer commitment which generates impressive bursts of language. Evident, too, is the amount of knowledge and experience children bring to the classroom which is often untapped by everyday work. Robert clearly has some understanding of aspects of animal cruelty picked up from books and parents: in this situation he becomes the 'expert' prepared to bring in examples of scientific language to back his ideas. There is not, in an adult sense, a logically worked-out sequence of ideas or polemic here. Robert's point about the cat being better off alive and blinded rather than dead might not bear scrutiny by the RSPCA, and his point about animals experimenting on us for rabies begs the question of the different status of human beings. Yet these kinds of empathetic, naive perceptions, though not perhaps mirroring adult, logical ways of thinking, present us with refreshingly new lateral lines of thought which combine thinking and feeling in ways only a child is capable of. Rather than try to expose the naivety of their views ('you'll understand these things when you're older') we should embrace them and encourage the children to develop from their committed stance. In painting and writing we would encourage exploration and adventure and would not be too critical of the end product. In 'Campaign' the children were in one sense 'daubing' with the rough draft of ideas in an atmosphere that was both sharing and challenging, open and rigorous. The picture of what they thought and felt was slowly emerging, blurred at first, clearer later, from the developing tray of their language.

In this they very much benefited from working with others, not only as a means of shaping and refining ideas, but because in discussing with other groups of individuals they could support each other. In the taped extract above the children do far more talking than the adult. This is rare. At key moments they chip in ideas together so that the persuasive effort becomes a collaborative one. Working together in this way they are not overawed by the adult, however many right answers and sophisticated arguments he or she tries to produce.

After the discussion phase of the first morning-and-a-half, groups began to focus their efforts beyond the classroom. What had perhaps begun as vague ideas brainstormed as part of a classroom exercise became real and significant as children wrote to newspapers, got parents to mass-produce pamphlets to distribute, arranged appointments with the head and the canteen supervisors to discuss bringing in a cafeteria system for the school. We were concerned that they should not be disappointed or disillusioned by the reception of their ideas in the big world outside. We did not want them to expect instant results and so we encouraged them instead to achieve goals such as getting a letter printed in the paper, alerting a Parish Council about a gap in facilities. But the outside world proved to be more positive and encouraging than we had imagined. The local paper ran features on two of the campaigns; a manager of a clothing firm who had received a leaflet from the group trying to set themselves up as teenage fashion designers, came to school to talk with them and examine their ideas; letters were published and replied to. One group who set up a campaign for more youth facilities for the area in order to reduce vandalism, progressed from a letter to the *Leicester Mercury*, a Parish Council meeting, and a mention on Radio Leicester, to a feature on Central TV in which they were interviewed. A month later a special Parish Council meeting which the girls attended set up two youth clubs in the area.

We were staggered by both the stamina and the broad range of views these ten-year-olds possessed. The key to the success of the activity seemed to us to be that they were working together on self-chosen issues which had a real outcome. The focus was entirely on the task, the purpose, the process. Lizzy summarised this well in her taped evaluation of the project:

> It was nice to work in a group and share ideas with each other and also to be able to write letters to people and show our views and get their views as well ... and I liked the way we were allowed to choose our campaigns because, if we didn't choose then we'd be doing something we didn't like and then it wouldn't be so much fun ...

The key to the generation of commitment here was that it was self-motivated and purposeful. Once we had set them going, our main problem was not keeping them at it, but trying both to control and to support the explosion of ideas and activities in the classroom. During the observation period I had noticed that much of the talk in the classroom had been 'off-task' chatter (sometimes called 'gossip'!) which helped to create a relaxed context for work, but which had little value in developing or extending ideas. During 'Campaign', though, the classroom was buzzing with purposeful talk; for the whole three days neither of us noticed a single example of 'off-task' chatter or desultory gossip.

Such intensity of involvement cannot be sustained throughout the week in a primary classroom. Work like this is perhaps best done in short, concentrated bursts in between calmer, more relaxed phases. That is not to say it should be isolated from the normal life of the classroom. We were aware that the campaign work offered the possibilities for purposeful learning of all kinds. Groups were highly motivated to learn how to set out letters, word pamphlets. The realisation that they needed to be well informed to be able to persuade others and fend off counter-arguments offered a valuable springboard for research into, for example, the pollution of canals in the area, or the use of vivisection. The work of the groups continued with the presentations of their campaigns to the whole class. The level of confidence and self-image was sufficiently high amongst the groups that they conducted these classroom sessions without the obvious help of the teachers who sat on the sidelines whilst the pupils invited discussion and replied to points made.

What did the children themselves think of all this and what did it have to do with their everyday learning? In a series of taped and written comments, most of them shared a remarkably sophisticated and understanding response to the work:

> It sort of taught us about life ... you'd know how to get at things and how to speak to people ... and you won't be so shy as you would be normally if you hadn't done anything like this at school.

> It got us thinking about what is going on in the world.

It was good for our education. We had to find out what people thought of our views and persuade them for our campaign ... it helped us to do what we felt strongly and get somewhere.

David's comments point to a purpose we had not considered:

It taught us something different that they don't teach you at school – how to kind of like, be active ... kind of like work together in a group and try to get a 'campaign' together ... You need to be active. It will help us to have our say in things when we are older.

I will do my best to ignore Phillipa's devastating comment that she enjoyed 'Campaign' ... but would rather get on with her work because she was particularly behind with her Fletcher Maths.

Generally the comments from these ten-year-olds were surprisingly sophisticated. It seemed the work had raised their consciousness about themselves and their status – the image they had of themselves as learners. They were in control of their own learning. In a very real sense they saw themselves as in the driving seat – the communicators who had a message to put across. They were pumped up with the pressure of ideas and, given an audience and a purpose, the talk flowed. It occurred to us that, for once, the children were the experts with something urgent to tell us. There had been a shift of stance between teachers and learners.

He won't know what a horse is

Subsequently I tried to follow up some of these ideas with a final-year infant class and their teacher in the same school. The teacher and I wanted to devise strategies whereby her class of seven-year-olds were put in the position of being 'experts', of having something to say. Pieces of evidence from this phase of work have already been referred to. Nigel's oral stories became increasingly successful as he began to see himself as a story-teller who had something to offer. The inventors of the fantastic machines were in a very real sense experts; no one else knew what the machines were and how they worked. The success of the discussion about He-Man with the two boys was largely due to the fact that I knew nothing about the series and could not therefore dominate the ideas or the flow of discussion. They had the store of ideas and I was empty. As air or water flows from high pressure areas to areas of low pressure so their talk flowed down the channel to me, the interested but ignorant audience.

Once the pupils are put in this more dominant position, where they have something to tell an interested, relatively ignorant audience, then the place of talk is guaranteed. But how credibly can we teachers consistently adopt this stance? Is it not true to say that the younger the learners the less they know, the more the teacher has to adopt an artificial and deceptive stance – in effect pretending not to know in order to create the audience for talk, and to open up the flow? What might be the long-term effect on the learners and their teachers taking up this position of deferred expertise?

An effective strategy that teachers can regularly adopt without putting themselves in a position which could undermine their credibility is to acknowledge pretence in a more creative way. Role-play is a very positive way to alter directly the balance of power in the classroom, so that the learners possess more of the knowledge, a greater slice of the classroom expertise.

In the following extract, I had been working with a group of seven-year-olds who had built a time machine with a large-scale building kit I had brought into the classroom. The idea was that this was the remains of a crashed time machine and if they could only put the bits back together again they could use the machine to travel to the times and the places of their choosing. After a deal of purposeful, constructive talk about various possible models for the machine, they built and 'tested' it.

On their first flight they arrived at a strange planet in the future. The first creature they met was a strange person looking remarkably like me but who couldn't see because eyes were no longer any use on the planet. (This was the trigger, the code to let them know that the role-play was beginning: I simply stared straight ahead without acknowledging their presence.) The children, in a position of expertise as I knew nothing about their planet, fell over themselves to tell me all about Earth. We began by talking about schools.

Alien: What do 'schools' mean?
Jill: Well schools are where you learn things.
Rosie: And you write.
Jill: You write and read and do lots of Maths.
Alien: What's writing?
Rosie: You take a pencil ... and ...
Jill: Then you sort of move it around doing shapes and they're the letters and that's how you write.
Rosie: You read words.
Jill: (*Showing a book*) These are the words you can read.
Rosie: And people have wrote them ... in ... and they become ... and they put a cover on them and that becomes a book and that's how you read other people's stories.

It began to emerge that the role-play was enabling them to be in a position where they could communicate their knowledge in a unique way. The alien was utterly and completely ignorant of the fundamentals of life on Earth. To fill this vacuum they had to review their past experience and give it shape for a new context. The tone and flavour of their approach is that of an adult talking to a very small child.

We roamed over matters of anatomy, birth, death and religion. (There was no death on the alien's planet.) The children told me Bible stories and explained about excretion which I thought was very messy and inefficient. In this extract they were explaining to me all about zoos and animals.

Alien: What are zoos?
Rosie: Well it's all this big ... *place* and it's ...
David: millions of cages ...
Rosie: yes ... and cages and these little huts with animals like crocodiles in it and they snap at you.
Alien: What's a cage?
Rosie: Well ... cages ...
David: There's all those metal ... er ... poles.
Rosie: Well ... no ... no ... David ... well it has this flat top, and then it has all metal bars around it.
Alien: Is it nice, living in there?
Jill: We don't know ... we live in houses.
Alien: Do you think the animals like living in the cages?
Various: Yes ... No ... They'd rather be free ...
Jill: You can't learn about them and you can't see them ... there you can look at them.
Rosie: Yes ... because they run so fast and hide.

With a minimum of steering from the adult the children are here able to transcend simple description and to begin to talk about some underlying issues. As in the 'Campaign' discussions they are benefiting greatly from their combined, collaborative approach to this ignorant but questioning alien. Together they can support each other and grow in confidence.

They go on to tell me about the individual animals, on an imaginary tour of the zoo.

Jill: That's a giraffe.
Alien: A what?
Jill: It's a giraffe
Alien: A *giraffe*.
Rosie: It's really tall ... it's got ...
Jill: a long neck ...
Rosie: it's got a body ...
Jill: It's like a horse, but with a long, long neck.
Rosie: Yes ... It's like ... no ... no ... he won't know what a horse is ... This ... it's flat like that, and then down here there's these legs, four legs and then you come back up here and then there's this tall neck and right at the top, there's a face something like us, but not the right ... exactly the same and then they have these horns and mouths so they can eat off the trees because they eat leaves and thorns.
Alien: Why's it got a long neck?
Rosie: So they can reach the leaves and thorns off the trees.
Jill: Because leaves are very high up in the trees and trees are things that grow from wood ... and wood is very strong ... but the giraffe can reach right up to the tree and eat the leaves, their food.

Their immersion in the imaginative world is here complete. The urgent rush of collaborative communication is marked by a sensitivity to audience and purpose. They were the teachers and I was the learner who did not know, for once, what a horse was.

The theme behind all this was time. This particular group were travelling in time. A rich variety of other activities were also available. Children could make sand-clocks, draw or construct their own clocks, play a computer time-telling game. Michael and Elaine chose to dismantle one of the broken clocks that had been brought into the classroom. They were left on their own in a withdrawal room and simply asked to see if they could find out how it worked. In this situation the two children were 'deprived' of any outside source of expertise and relied instead on their own ideas. There was no pool of knowledge available to refer to or defer to ... their own image of themselves was of enquiring, curious scientists and their language reflected this view of themselves. Some way into the discussion, Elaine has a breakthrough:

Elaine: I know now ... what happens is you wind this up ...
Michael: Yes.
Elaine: You wind up that key and that coil round there gets tighter ... and then it starts to unwind very very slowly and the clock hands ... go ... turn round.
Michael: What about all these other little cogs and springs?
Elaine: Hold on ... wait ... don't ... I think I've got it.
Michael: What ... this moves ...
Elaine: I know.
Michael: Do you think it will move ... I suppose it's always possible.
Elaine: Could I just ... ah! It must be that that turns it ... yes it's ... so if I was to stop that from turning.
Michael: Could I sit where you are ... shall we swap?
Elaine: No ... you have a good old peek at the other side ... wait ... Ha! Ha! I think I know how it works. Wait, don't turn it a minute, Michael ... This clock is extremely strict about what it's doing.
Michael: Yes ... all clocks are ... well they're supposed to be ... maybe it's a good old one ... interesting how that moves. If you stop it the whole clock will stop ...
Elaine: Yes ... but if you stop *that* the whole clock will stop.
Michael: Yes ... but if we stop all of them ... if we stop just one gear the whole clock will stop.
Elaine: Yeah ... I know.

It is important that the two children are working on their own here, away from the stifling clutches of adult expertise and manipulation. In these circumstances they are free to speculate, to rehearse, examine closely, theorise, test their ideas and to use a free-ranging, creative running commentary of talk as the medium of their explorations. Note, too, how the *object* serves as a focus in a way that a picture and diagram never could. They have something real, something tangible to centre their talk on. There is something to talk about which they can also look at and handle. It is interesting, too, that Elaine is very much a dominant partner in this 'scientific' investigation to the plaintive Michael. I noticed this elsewhere in the classroom. It could well be that, at least at this age, girls are less overawed in the more open and creative learning situations than in more closed tasks.

Work in the secondary schools during the same term confirmed the strong impression I had formed in these two primary classrooms that changing the stance of the learners, giving the learners the feel that they were in control of the learning and were in a position of greater expertise meant that they were much more ready to explore ideas and express themselves through talk than they would be if they were in a position of relative ignorance.

The investigation

In a first-year (11-year-old) Science classroom the teacher set up a piece of investigative work in which groups of children worked as forensic scientists analysing pieces of evidence from the scene of a murder. On the basis of their results they had to deduce whom they thought was the prime suspect. Once a group had formed a conclusion, I confronted them in role as the lawyer for the accused and demanded to have precise accounts and explanations of their evidence. These groups of 11-year-olds, strong in their image of themselves as 'mini-scientists', faced my barrage of questions with unflinching confidence. Here is an exchange with one boy (whose written work was on this occasion criticised as a bit vague and lacking detail):

Teacher: It's my right as a lawyer to question you forensic scientists before the evidence appears in court. Now what evidence have you got to make this appalling accusation against my client?

Sean: In the tests we conducted on the soil samples, the fingerprints and the ink pen, it showed positive for her and it was negative for all the others.

Teacher: I want you to explain each test to me in detail because I'm going to be questioning these in a court of law. Start off with the soil.

Sean: We had soil samples from each of the suspect's shoes. We ground it up with a mortar and pestle and then we looked at them and hers was the only colour close to the soil found in the room.

Teacher: You just *looked* at them ... doesn't all dirt look the same?

Sean: We ground it ... and then because it was close, took the pH.

Teacher: Look, I'm not a scientist ... I don't know what a pH is.

Sean: Ah, well ... it's the universal indicator reading ... You dip the universal indicator in a diluted solution of soil and water and the indicator paper goes a colour and then you match the colour up to the colour in the table.

Teacher: What does that show besides colour?

Sean: The acidity or alkali of it ... the acidity of the soil we found in the room was pH4 and the soil from her shoe was pH4 also ...

The messages of the role-play have encouraged Sean here to launch into a fluent explanation and confirmation of his learning. His image of himself is sufficiently confident and the purpose for communication sufficiently strong for him to use language in a beautifully precise and controlled way. The contexts of the role-play has given shape, definition and purpose to his talk.

What I am saying here is that the fruitful use of learning-talk in the classroom is dependent on a change in methodology. It is in a sense a symptom of a transformed attitude to teaching and learning. If we teachers can make this transformation, this shift in stance, then we can at last begin to build some of the insights of educationalists over the last twenty years into our everyday classrooms.

Two cautionary tales

Old habits die hard. The vestiges of former models of learning, the blueprints of the previous history of our teaching, linger far beyond their philosophical rejection. We must not be lured into thinking that once we have got the theory right, then our classrooms will be transformed. This is the assumption that has so dogged education and has led to what I see as a huge gap between the theory of what we perhaps ought to be doing and the practice of the everyday experience of the learner in the classroom.

An observation of a block of work in a first-year Science class serves to illustrate this point. It was a very carefully prepared and well-delivered package of work, of the kind very common in the 1970s, designed to set groups of children up in experimental, investigative work. The work was tightly structured but ostensibly open-ended. The pupils had to find out through practical investigations which of three samples of water was most polluted. Sets of needed equipment were readily available, as were bottles of sample A (cloudy), sample B (containing a few twigs and leaves) and sample C (completely clear). A worksheet asked for three tests:

1 A visual check.
2 A test by which each sample was put in a test tube and shaken. The pupils then timed how long it took for the resulting bubbles to disappear.
3 A filtration.

Various groups of pupils worked steadily through the experiments, chattering busily about trainers and friends as they did so. At the end of the session they all had the same result. The teacher had had serious doubts about the nature of the learning that was going on in this kind of work and had asked me to monitor the work through observation of the talk going on, and by talking with the pupils about what they had perceived through the lesson. It became clear that though this was a 'successful' piece of work in terms of the orderly procession through a series of experiments to reach the 'right' conclusions, it had not really engaged the brains or the imaginations of the pupils in any significant sense. The exercise was too given, too closed. Rather than being mini-scientists, who had expertise to offer, the pupils were deferring to the implied knowledge of the worksheet. The sheet had acted as a teacher-presence, guiding its audience towards what they should be thinking and the results they should achieve. Any valuable scientific thought-processes were thereby pre-empted.

What the pupils needed in order to enhance their image of themselves and hence liberate the full flow of their ideas and commitment was a much more open, process-based approach. What we should have done was present them with the samples, and asked them in groups to devise three separate tests to compare pollution levels. These tests could then have been discussed and explored in the whole class and then carried out (within limitations of available equipment) by the individual groups. In keeping with the notion of handing the expertise over to the pupils, any writing-up to be done could take the form of the report from a group of technicians asked to monitor relative pollution levels.

Any feelings of smugness I might have been developing from my observations of other people's lessons were severely dented when I reviewed the tapes I had made in the final-year junior class of primary school some time later. The teacher and I had decided that the children needed the chance to speculate and hypothesise without the constraint of right or wrong answers. We then set up a piece of work in which we told them what we were going to do in an experiment and asked them to try to predict what might happen. We would then demonstrate the experiment and they would try to create fresh explanations in the light of what they had observed happening. In the experiment we were going to bring a small amount of water to the boil in a large tin can and then screw the top on and take it off the boil. We knew that it was important to stress that we were not so much interested in right answers as in their ability to form theories and suggest credible scientific explanations. The first hint that both pupils and teachers have difficulty escaping from their traditional roles came when one group explained their theory to the teacher and asked if they were right. 'I'm not going to make any comment. I'm just interested in your ideas,' said the teacher. 'I can tell we are wrong from the tone of your voice,' replied a girl in the group.

In the experiment we eventually demonstrated that steam replaced most of the air inside the can of boiling water and when the can was taken off the heat, it cooled, the steam condensed and air-pressure collapsed the sides. In the subsequent whole-class discussion I realised that, against all our intentions, we found ourselves lapsing back almost irresistibly into the 'teacher-as-expert-with-right-answer' model as the following extract shows:

Teacher: Why did the sides cave in?
Nick: Is it because it's sucking in the oxygen?
Teacher: What's sucking in what oxygen?
Nick: The steam.
Teacher: Hmm! What do you think, Stephen?
Stephen: Well, the heat needs the oxygen and it's sucking the oxygen in which makes the sides go in because there is no more oxygen.
Teacher: Hmm! Let's see if anyone can come up with a slightly different explanation. Mark?
Mark: There's no oxygen to keep the tin from going in.
David: Vacuum.
Teacher: Ah! What was that word, David?
David: Vacuum.
Teacher: Good.

We had been reared as teachers, as leaders of children towards adult knowledge. This role had asserted itself in the discussion above in which we were guiding and steering the children towards the 'right' answer. There is a place for such discussions in schools, of course. But *not* in a lesson where our clear intention was to encourage the children to speculate freely, untrammelled by the notion that the main aim was to arrive at the right answer.

Teachers must be very clear-headed in their intentions as to what they want to achieve through talk in the classroom. They must thoroughly understand the circumstances in which learning-talk will flower and those which will cause it to wither. To achieve this they must re-examine their stance as educators of young people and be prepared to monitor their own performances in the light of their aims. Much of this is a question of vigorous self-awareness which can be painful at times. Only if teachers are prepared to ask the right questions about *themselves* (as well as of the learners) can they begin to make that difficult transformation. The fate of talk in schools hinges round our answers to two fundamental questions, the ones which underlie so many issues in education but which are rarely asked and hardly ever answered by curriculum constructors: What is learning? What are schools for?

If our answer to the first question tallies with that of the ten-year-old who told me that 'learning is storing facts in your head' then I suspect we can order plenty of paper and reference books and rest content. If instead we embrace the interpretative view posed by Britton (1970b) and Barnes (1976) and see learning as the act of reshaping the new in the light of experience of the old, then it becomes necessary to involve the learner actively in that process, and talk would seem to be the most natural, flexible and economical way of doing so. If learning thereby becomes the negotiation of new realities for the learner, then the most direct medium for that negotiation is talk, though certain kinds of writing can achieve the same purpose for some pupils.

If schools are merely places designed to transmit 'stuff' to pupils' heads from books or from teachers' heads, then there may be more efficient ways of doing this than having pupils talk together; though I would argue that even in this poverty-stricken model of education, talk is the best way to develop and confirm understanding. If, however, schools wish to be places which offer the learner a chance to grow, and to develop certain qualities – qualities such as curiosity, flexibility, the ability to communicate with and work with other people, the wish to have one's say in the shaping of the world and to acquire the means to do so – then talk comes to the centre of the learning experience rather than shyly peeping over the fence at the extreme periphery.

Ultimately our view of talk in schools depends on our philosophy of education, our personal, some would say political, judgement on how we can best serve the young people in our care.

PART FIVE

Overview

10 The changing context

There can be no curriculum change without teacher change.
Laurence Stenhouse

So far a number of points have been made about appropriate and inappropriate contexts for learning-talk. These are summarised in Table 5. Read through the list on the left-hand side. If you are a teacher, is your classroom and teaching approach reflected there? More importantly are the factors *within your control*? If your answer is at least a reserved 'yes' to both of these questions I am prepared to assert that you are likely either to be a primary or middle school teacher or that you are a secondary school teacher who is to some extent deceiving him- or herself.

I shall clearly have to come back to that. For the moment let us try the following 'exercise'. During 1985–6 I spent a year in one family of schools: a 5–11 primary school; an 11–14 secondary school; and a 14–18 upper school. During two terms I spent a total of 73 days in the schools, a total of 24 in two primary classrooms, the remaining time being roughly equally divided between the two secondary schools. I worked in a variety of ways – as observer, auxiliary helper and classroom teacher. In this way I gathered a vast amount of 'evidence' in the form of quantitative analysis, questionnaire results, subjective diary-style reflections, tape recordings of classroom work and interviews with pupils and teachers, bits and pieces of children's written and oral work and a host of other things. Below is a selection from that evidence. Some of it has been referred to already; most is new pieces of evidence, picked at random from the files of material collected. Looking at each extract in turn, please decide for yourself whether it points towards a fruitful context for learning-talk, or an unpromising one (see Table 5). Mark each, if you like with a 'F' or a 'U', or a '?' if you are unsure about it. I know that in practice you would want to see the full context of the extract before pronouncing, but suspend those thoughts and be prepared to be 'crude' for the moment.

1 'The morning was a busy, active one with a wide variety of language activities around. The room was filled with talk' (from field notes).

Table 5. Contexts for learning-talk.

Context	Effect on learning-talk	
	Encourage	Discourage
Physical	Desks in groups or U-shape	Desks in rows
	Good acoustics	Poor acoustics
	Cassette players available	No equipment
	Extended time available	Limited time available
Personal	Warm, open relationship with teacher	Distant, suspicious relationship with teacher
	Secure non-competitive relationships with peers	Insecure, competitive peer group relationships
	Relaxed, accepting atmosphere	Tense, aggressive atmosphere
	Pupils have strong self-image as learners	Pupils have low self-image as learners
Task	Open	Closed
	Active involvement sought	Passivity expected
	A purposeful outcome	No clear purpose or outcome
	Real objects and tasks at the centre	Purely abstract exercises
	Tasks require collaboration	Tasks done individually
Pedagogy	Pupils' contribution most important	Teacher's contribution most important
	Small groups, pupil-led	Whole class, teacher-led
	Learning to *do* things	Learning things
	Process-based curriculum	Content-based curriculum
	Talk a valid part of learning	Talk peripheral
	Starting where the pupils are at	Starting where the teacher is at
	Teacher as learning expert	Teacher as subject expert
	Pupils have autonomy	Pupils have no autonomy
	Pupils influence agenda-for-learning	Teacher dictates agenda-for-learning
	Clear, understood approach to talk	Teacher confused

2 'Basically the idea was to measure the forces necessary to pull a kilogram weight up an increasing slope. You increase the slope by placing bricks at one end of a board and then we just pulled it up with a newton meter, and measured the force in newtons. We recorded the average in our books ... we did it up to six bricks and when we got to six bricks, it took $7\frac{1}{2}$ newtons to pull up. The two forces really are gravity and friction preventing it to move' (taped interview with Michael).

3 *Alastair:* I think the water, when it boils comes to the boil ... the bubbles may expand and make the tin expand ... or the steam may turn to fumes from the smell in the can.

  Teacher: That's interesting.

  Anne: I think it's going to expand as well, because that's what happened to my sister's Tipp-Ex bottle when she put it in warm water (taped extract from lesson).

4 Caroline: 'If you want to learn something, you've got to know the right answer ... and if you're in little groups, you've perhaps not got the teacher with you to tell you that you're right or wrong about something.'

5 'Arriving at ten minutes to nine the classroom is already buzzing with activity. A hand slips into mine, pulls me along: "Come and meet my robot ..."' (diary).

6 'When I saw you going round talking to the kids, I felt "I should be doing that". I have to spend most of my time giving out paper and keeping an eye on the naughty ones' (teacher's comment to me).

7 'He has a test in Maths. The teacher spends ten minutes carefully introducing the work. Martin gets increasingly restless. I sense a rise in temperature, a build-up of his more negative impulses. Suddenly, out of the blue he scribbles on the worksheet of the boy opposite, just seconds after the teacher had said "Please don't write on the sheets"' (field notes on a 'pupil-day').

8 'There is real autonomy here: the kids make their own choices and are responsible for their own materials. A small group made a hash of mixing the powdered glue. The teacher watched them do it and then suggested that they read the instructions and worked out how to measure a half litre accurately' (field notes).

9 'John explained what the video was going to be about. Ivan shouts "What's it about? ... I've seen it before anyway"' (field notes on a 'pupil-day').

10 *Teacher:* Of course, as rivers flow down towards the sea they carry with them large quantities of what? Not just water, but large quantities of ...?

  Boy: Stuff and rubbish?

11 'The centres of interest round the clock display and computer were helpful and several pairs of pupils seemed to be working together quite naturally around them. Two girls worked on the computer overlooked by a mixed group of two or three making comments. Two boys were writing a story together in another corner of the room' (field notes).

12 'The teacher had to create very quickly a short-hand version of his expectations – in this strange class he didn't know very many names, let alone personalities. He had to 'change hats' very quickly and tell them he was prepared to punish anyone who spoiled the atmosphere' (diary).

13 'I thought it was good because it was to do with Maths and it was fun.

It gave us all the chance to give each other our ideas by setting problems for other friends, the same age as us. It made us think about Maths' (written comment from pupils evaluating a Maths lesson).

14 *Time analysis: the activity of one pupil in one session*

Waiting and setting-up	10 mins
Listening to teacher	28 mins
Read to by teacher	4 mins
Watching video	19 mins
Chatting (lesson finished early)	4 mins
	65 mins

15 'I prefer school to home. There's more to do here' (taped comment from Elizabeth).

I am going to open myself to the charge of being unfair by revealing where the 'evidence' came from. Numbers (1), (3), (5), (8), (11), (13) and (15) were from the primary stage and the rest from the secondary schools. If you have shared my views about the nature of fruitful learning-talk and helpful learning contexts you will notice, I suspect, a high correlation between the primary stage and likely examples of good learning.

To be a little more specific, in (1) the notion of a whole morning's coherent, active work is very much a primary one. In (2) Michael is, however articulately, rehearsing a common experiment, with common aims and results. There's a touch of bored certainty in his utterances. Alastair and Anne in (3) are being more tentative, speculative and personal in their approach to Science whilst the teacher remains interested and open. (4) reveals a teacher-dependent notion of right and wrong, so destructive to the image of the learners. The relaxed, personal, atmosphere of (5) implies an excellent context for learning. But the secondary teachers in (6) and (12) feel themselves clenched in the twin jaws of authority and administration. The sense of negative and hostile alienation from learning in (7) and (9) makes a contrast with natural commitment and involvement in (11) and (15). (8) reveals a much more child-centred learning model in which mistakes are a natural part of learning, whereas in (10) there is a teacher-led straining for correct responses to a content-based curriculum. In (14) we see the standard pattern of many secondary subject sessions. The children are led around the content on the display and view it passively from different angles, working as a whole class. The collaborative enjoyment and intellectual challenge evident in (13) speaks of a more purposeful and involved experience.

All highly selective, of course, but I ask you to trust me that the above is a fair reflection of my experience amongst a variety of schools and age ranges. Whether we are considering talk or the whole spectrum of learning activity, I am forced to conclude that primary schools offer much more fruitful opportunities for 'real learning' than secondary schools.

The story of my experience of primary schools is that the vast majority *an illusion* of them are open, warm and accepting places where confidence flowers and individuals are given the space to grow. It is difficult to quote hard-and-fast evidence for this; I can only report the symptoms and signposts which lead me towards this instinctive judgement. Children, in the main, enjoy going there. 'There's more to do here', says Elizabeth, who preferred school to home. Learning is an enjoyable experience for her. She is still carried forward by the momentum of her instinctive curiosity to find things out, to explore the world. The school experience gives her the opportunity to do so, to make mistakes on the way and to learn through a personal journey. The classroom begins from where she is at, from what she brings to it. Her relationship with the teacher is secure and warm; the teacher knows her parents well and they are welcome in the classroom at the beginning of the day if there is a problem which can be discussed briefly. There is continuity between the home and school experience. Indeed adults of all kinds appear in the classroom and are accepted as a natural part of the environment. And when they do come they must perforce become part of the classroom resource, hearing stories, commenting on paintings, tearing up newspaper for papier-mâché. All this creates the right environment for learning and for learning-talk in particular. Elizabeth's class is, I believe, more than just a model of a talk-conducive classroom; it stands for the majority of primary classrooms I have encountered. There are, of course, classrooms up and down the country that would deny this and offer an opposite experience. It would be true to say that Elizabeth's class has its more formal moments and days when children are flogging through sums together or copying up stories. The teacher, too, can get angry and shout. That is all part of the human experience. But I would be prepared to assert that there are significantly more primary classrooms operating this kind of open model of learning than there are ones offering the closed, transmission-based kind, still so common in secondary schools.

Primary teachers are frustratingly diffident about all this. If anything they feel that their secondary colleagues have all the expertise and are much 'further ahead'. They tend to see themselves as journeymen and women rather than professionals. They could not be further from the truth. The fundamental difference is that secondary teachers see themselves as subject experts, to whom a little knowledge about learning is useful in putting content across; whereas primary teachers see themselves as learning experts to whom a little knowledge about subjects is useful in enabling their pupils to learn.

One of the curriculum phrases current in secondary education during 1986–7 was 'active learning'. This 'new' idea, on which hundreds of thousands of pounds were spent on in-service work, aimed to enable the pupils to have a more active and less passive learning experience; they needed to be actively engaged in real tasks undertaken collaboratively. No more would they sit in rows, absorbing (or deflecting) content. So what is so new about that? Primary school teachers took these messages on board years ago.

This book is not based on formal 'research', but on experience supported by small-scale enquiry; these are just my stories. Parts of them may be dismissed as unrepresentative fiction; but it is my strong conviction that they point to the truth and that secondary teachers urgently need to learn from them. The primary school experience is by no means a completely coherent or continuous one (it depends crucially on who your teachers are). It would seem to me that the open and active learning situations I have encountered amongst six- and seven-year-olds is progressively narrowed so that by the age of ten the learning experience is a more formal one. The classes seem to work together more as a whole, centring round greater chunks of skills-based and topic-based work. This 'regression' of the learning experience in final-year junior classrooms is largely due to the deference of the primary school teachers to the secondary experience, against what I believe to be their own best instincts. As one teacher put it: 'I've got to get them used to subjects and more written work. Otherwise they'll not cope when they go up to the big school.'

So the transition to secondary schools is, by virtue of the sensitivity and compromise of final-year junior teachers, less of a precipice and more of a large step at the end of a downward slope. I use the word 'downward' advisedly. Looked at from the standpoint of the perceived consensus of educational theory about how learning best happens, it would be true to say that the learning experience steadily deteriorates from the age of seven onwards, with a particularly marked regression after the age of 11. I would go so far as to say that children actually *unlearn* particular qualities and abilities as they move through the system. The tragedy is that many of these qualities and abilities are ones which teachers value strongly and pay lipservice to fostering in their classrooms. I should like to illustrate these sweeping assertions by examining particular classroom issues that throw them into perspective.

Children working together

As a secondary English teacher I am constantly trying to create strategies to get pupils working together in pairs or small groups. Whole in-service courses are devoted to this end. If I get the strategy and the task right then I can succeed, but it gets harder and harder as the pupils get older. Fifteen-year-olds can often be quite resistant to exchanging ideas with others and can actively resist joint work. Once the 'coursework folder' mentality has taken over and pupils are working pretty well exclusively for final exams then working together becomes in one sense a form of cheating rather than a source of support.

In the primary classroom not only is classroom furniture organised to emphasise collaboration and sharing (children sit together in clusters) but the whole climate is such that it is natural, indeed necessary, to work together in a variety of ways – consulting, sharing, making models, writing and experimenting together. They do this without the constant prompting of the teacher and without the need for creating elaborate (and sometimes gimmicky) strategies. Children unlearn how to work creatively together.

Curiosity

How many of us have explained to our classes in the secondary school that they need to ask questions if they do not understand? How many of them do? How many of them have experienced what my youngest son did at the age of 11, when he asked a Maths teacher about a particular process he did not understand and was shouted at? (He says he will never, ever, ask another question in Maths.) If learning is understanding what the teacher is transmitting then 'I don't understand' becomes an implicit criticism of that teacher's technique. If learning is enabling the learner to come to terms with his or her own reality then to ask questions is an essential part of the process. Very young children have a natural curiosity. They touch, taste, smell everything within their grasp and when language later emerges it becomes a key tool in finding out more. From the age of three or four the natural tendency of children is to bombard the adult with questions, real questions, to which they want to know the answers. From the age of 11 it is the teacher who is bombarding the children with questions, pseudo-questions to which the answer is already known. Children unlearn that essentially curious, questioning attitude to the world that they have at the age of five. With the demise of curiosity comes the loss of enjoyment of learning and the drying up of the commitment to find out.

Attitudes to others

Galton and Anning (1986) reported that they perceived sexist and racist attitudes amongst pupils in the primary school. I have to say that during my time in infant classrooms I came across no such clear evidence. There may have been isolated incidents that I missed, but for every one of those there must have been a dozen more positive experiences where young children from mixed class and ethnic backgrounds were working together untrammelled by the attitudes that so clearly pervade the secondary school. Other children are accepted as people to work with, talk to, learn from, as are other adults. Because I was so used to male-dominated secondary classrooms, when I encountered the equality and mixed groupings of the primary classroom I was tempted to believe that they were in fact girl-dominated. Certainly the girls more than held their own and were often the leaders in classroom activity. Michael's plaintive comment to Elaine in

Chapter 9: 'Could I sit where you are – shall we swap?' as he tries to get a piece of the learning action, would not be echoed in very many secondary Science classrooms. Primary school children are not as blinkered or inhibited in their responses to other huuman beings as secondary pupils are. It was certainly my impression, as it is of very many secondary teachers, that sexist and racist behaviour becomes an increasingly serious and overt problem as pupils get older. Children, then, unlearn their open and accepting views of other people. This has profound implications for their use of talk for learning.

Autonomy

Included amongst the long-term goals of many school prospectuses and departmental statements of aims is a commitment to the development of autonomy in the learner. The conventional wisdom would have it that as children begin to grasp concepts, skills and ways of working, so they can be expected to take more and more responsibility for their own learning. Ideally by the age of 16 they emerge as autonomous learners equipped for life with the tools for self-education; in reality, nothing could be further from the truth. It may be that such a goal as the development of the responsible self-planning learner may be partly realised at the end of some more forward-looking A level courses. But for many pupils staying at school beyond the statutory minimum period, such a goal is receding rather than approaching, depressed as it is by the great weight of given content at 16 + and the associated didactic teaching methods.

My impression whilst observing secondary classes across the curriculum is that the pupils are increasingly teacher-dependent as they progress through the system, inexorably shedding what autonomy they had at the end of the primary phase. In five separate pupil pursuits I undertook in the secondary phase, over 70 per cent of the observed teacher–pupil interaction was at a merely administrative level, requesting equipment, defining the exact nature of the tasks. Teachers in secondary classrooms seem to spend an unacceptable proportion of their time issuing paper, finding scissors, writing out lengthy notes giving permission to go to the library. The most cynical observer could interpret this as a studied avoidance of the more demanding and hence more threatening activity of the meeting of minds. There is simply no *tradition* of autonomous learning in the secondary school. Expert teachers have things to put across to ignorant learners and they are preoccupied not only with serving up the knowledge but with providing all the tools and materials the learners need. No doubt they are severely hampered by a number of practical considerations. If teachers have their own rooms and their own equipment stocks, for example, then they can accustom pupils if they wish to the resources of the rooms and encourage them to be less teacher-dependent. But to give each teacher his or her own room would only aid, not ensure, the transformation of autonomy. At the root, behind the superficial detail, is the question of the learning model: What is learning? What are schools for?

Suffice to say that I have observed more autonomy in the majority of infant classrooms I have encountered than in the majority of upper secondary classrooms. Certainly, seven-year-olds are less dependent on teachers for mere material needs. They know where the paper and paints are and at most need to ask permission to use them. The logistics of the activity-based classroom dictate that this be so. Even in the matter of choice – the second step towards autonomy beyond the merely administrative – the seven-year-olds are better served than their secondary counterparts. It is common for 15-year-olds to have *no* choice and to simply be working through a topic as a class at the dictate of the officer (teacher) or NCO (worksheet).

Where there is choice it tends to show itself in choice between activities at the same level (such as a list of titles for stories). Rare indeed is the provision of a variety of activities, possibly related in theme but distinct in the nature of the task. Where in the secondary school would I find as rich a variety of possible activities as Nigel had to choose from when he told his robot story: he could have painted or constructed robots, read or written about them, experimented with or made actual working models, or played a computer game. All this was available that day alongside such bread-and-butter tasks as his English or Maths work. I am not implying that uncontrolled anarchy prevailed, though anarchy has much to recommend it and is, I suspect, the least understood of the range of life-views available to us. No, in good primary classrooms there is a kind of joint control between teacher and learners. The teacher creates the framework and may make specific demands (you must do some of this or some of that during the week), but in general the learner has more freedom to follow his or her natural learning rhythms through guided choice in the primary classroom than in the secondary classroom. The implications for commitment to learning and the use of talk for learning are profound. A simplified diagrammatic representation of this regression might resemble Figure 1. Seven-year-olds seem in my experience to have been given more *trust* than 15-year-olds and from that early expectation flows a greater sense of commitment and responsibility. Children begin to unlearn this at the transfer stage and the process is pretty well complete at 16.

Expressive talk

Writers about language and learning have stressed for the last 20 years the need for pupils to be given the chance to talk about their learning in a way that has come to be labelled as expressive. Peter Medway's (1984, p. 155) notes on this will serve as a useful definitive. He characterises the expressive

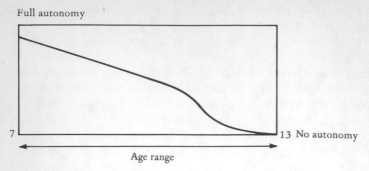

Figure 1. Pupil dependence on teachers

with a number of features: 'Communication (of information and ideas) inextricably mixed with expression (of self and affect); assumption of the listener's/reader's interest in the speaker/writer as a person; absence of a felt need for strict accuracy or for tight logic or coherence; responsiveness to the changing direction and emphases of thought.'

In brief, this is the exploratory, collaborative, personal kind of talk described earlier in this book where the learner follows the contours of the mind and journeys beyond to reach out for fresh insights. Infants talk readily, constantly, in this mode. Indeed, when devising strategies for extending the talk of the seven-year-old infants in the class I worked with during 1986 the teacher and I sought ways of giving them talk opportunities *other than* the purely expressive (the exercise of making a machine and giving a formal explanation of how it worked was one example of this). By the end of the secondary phase this natural tendency has largely dried up, though I do not deny that a number of talented and committed teachers have created oases in individual classrooms.

It is likely that this pattern of a deterioration of learning opportunities is not just confined to the British educational system. In 1985 the results of a four-year study of Australian schools, *Children's Choice*, revealed that the use of oral language skills – involving such activities as conversation between individual pupils and teachers, small-group discussion, oral reading and story-telling – declined considerably as the pupils passed through the grades.

I can sense the hackles rising at this stage. The age-old defences are being prepared: 'It's all very well for infant and primary teachers. The children are naturally more curious and responsive. By the time they get to us they are much more hardened and difficult to manage. We have our work cut out simply keeping them in order and following the syllabus.' There is no doubt a lot of truth in this. Adolescents create more obvious difficulties and teachers are constrained by the demands of content-based syllabuses in the fourth and fifth years. But how much of this is an insurmountable barrier and how much an excuse behind which teachers can hide in defence of the continuation of less challenging and demanding teaching/learning models? Why do teachers of first to third years trot out the same excuses about covering content when in reality these years are unconstrained by formal syllabuses and examination outcomes? Is the gradual waning of enthusiasm and commitment to learning evidenced in secondary schools as the pupil regresses from the first year inevitable? Is the commonly-lamented 'third-year rot' an inescapable consequence of the chemical and biological changes of puberty? Are schools and teachers powerless to arrest this degeneration that I perceive in the attitude of the learners and hence in the learning experience itself? Are we completely at the mercy of physiological and social changes?

I suspect schools and teachers are more responsible for this decline than we care to admit. Determinism is too comfortable a refuge. Refer to my list at the beginning of this chapter of the appropriate and inappropriate contexts for learning-talk. Would it be roughly true to say that the 'encouraging' features largely describe primary schools and the 'discouraging' features refer in the main to secondary schools? I believe so, and if you share my belief, let me follow this up with another question. How many of the factors which discourage learning-talk are *inevitable* in the secondary schools? Do the desks *have* to be in rows. Does the timetable have to split learning up into fragmented gobbets of time? Is it essential that content dominates the curriculum so overwhelmingly? We can indeed reasonably challenge the inevitability of *all* those discouraging factors. I suspect that any secondary school with the collective will to do so could overcome these problems overnight, in that such things as furniture, timetables and content-based curricula could be rearranged. But these relatively accessible factors are not the most important ones. It will be clear from what I have said so far that the most stubborn agent in this drying-up of the learning experience is the vision that the school and the teachers have of learning and of learners.

It is evidently true that young babies from a very early age are pitch-perfect, can swim, avoid crawling over precipices, can grip things sufficiently to carry their own body weight. During their first two years of life these abilities are gradually unlearned. I would venture that the same could be said of certain key qualities in five-year-olds (such as the ability to use expressive talk for learning), that schools are in theory trying to foster. Perhaps these qualities and abilities are simply imprisoned within the learner and that if we work hard at it we can find the key to unlock them. My premise is simply that the way schools and classrooms work at the secondary level, pupils are deprived of this most valuable tool for learning. Until teachers undergo a fundamental change of heart, a radical shift of attitude, this will continue to be the case.

11 Tearing down the wall

> The first task of education is to destroy the tyranny of localism over the imagination.
>
> Bertrand Russell

I will try to finish this book on a positive and encouraging note. We know what the experts say we should be doing and we know that we are not doing enough. We have acknowledged the barriers to using learning-talk that face teachers and tried to tease out what the right contexts for that talk are – in terms of classroom environment, teaching model and learning task. Bearing in mind my conviction that if talk is to take its rightful place in the classroom there must be a fundamental shift in the attitude of teachers, what can be done in schools to effect this change?

The individual teacher

If you are a teacher, this book is writing about *you*, not the person teaching next to you. It is *you*, and I, who are denying the learners access to real learning through talk, not someone comfortably outside your existence. Fundamentally this is a matter of self-awareness.

Clearing your head

Ask yourself, what am I doing in my classroom that discourages learning-talk? Wipe the slate of your experience clean and start again with a long, hard look at your whole outlook and methodology. Ask yourself:

- What do my pupils *really* need to know?
- What do I mean by 'know'? Remember? Understand?
- What qualities/skills/abilities and attitudes should the pupils be developing in my classroom?
- How, then, can my aims be best achieved and in particular what part can talk play in achieving them?

Clarify in your mind what it is you want to achieve, and what kind of teacher you need to be. That is your essential base for your next, more painful journey.

Looking at yourself

Now take a hard and objective look at what actually happens from day to day in your classroom. Pair up with a colleague. Can he or she join you for a 'lesson'? Can the head be persuaded to regard your working in this way as legitimate in-service work, meriting supply cover? In any case it is enormously valuable to be working with a trusted colleague, prepared to join you on the journey. Decide on a framework of observation, a focus, and observe each other at work. The observer will need to be just a little detached from the work of the class and be prepared to jot notes down as things proceed. Particular focuses you might use are:

● The amount of talking done by the teacher compared to the pupils.
● The role of the teacher in any talk that does take place (including small-group work).
● The kind and nature of questions asked by the teacher and the learners.
● The kind and nature of pupil talk. Is it extended talk (what Gillian Brown calls 'long turns') or brief responses? Are the pupils exploring new ideas, exchanging views, explaining concepts, describing what they see? Is the agenda for discussion open or closed?
● The attitudes of the pupils to the talk in a lesson (useful here to prepare a short questionnaire to be completed in the last five minutes of the session. A follow-up taped interview with a selection of pupils can be very revealing too).

Whatever the focus, it is best to give the observer time to write up reflections at home in reflective tranquillity rather than to give hasty feedback immediately at the end of the session. The more expressive and freewheeling diary is the least threatening form, and one more conducive to the more tentative and open-ended approach necessary in a joint exploration. The diary can be shared and the teacher can add in her own perceptions.

Then reverse the roles. After a number of sessions it should be possible to decide on particular ways your teaching should be shifted as a result of the observation and reflections. Pick out specifics to be implemented, for example: 'I must never talk longer than five minutes: I must not "foreclose" or constantly comment on and reinterpret pupil contributions: I need to ask more questions I don't know the answer to.'

You could then arrange a further observation session both to monitor the effect of these changes and to focus on fresh aspects.

Pupil pursuit

It is an eye-opening exercise to follow a pupil through a day's lessons, experiencing things as they do. You will need to arrange cover to do so (supply?) but it will pay dividends in terms of your own insights into the learning experience. You will need to plan well in advance and ask the permission of everyone including the pupil you are to follow. Do not make either teacher or pupil feel over-scrutinised as this may 'skew' the exercise. Explain instead that you are simply trying to get the feel of what it is like to be a pupil, which is generally true. On the way, you will no doubt note important aspects of teacher and pupil behaviour that affect talk but do not do so crudely or obviously.

It is best to sit somewhere near the pupil, not necessarily next to him or her, but angled slightly towards him or her and somewhat away from the teacher, to remove both from your obvious gaze. Have a specific *focus* for the day (for example, how much talking does this pupil do and for what purposes?). This will give direction to your attention. If you can, join in the work of the class whilst making the odd note. It is best to write up experiences in diary form later, to confirm and sharpen up any insights you have had.

Studying pupil talk

Whether or not you are working with a colleague it is a fairly straight-forward matter to make tapes of everyday classroom talk. It is hard to make a good-quality tape of a whole-class session – but at least *your* contributions will be heard (including your questions). It is easier to tape a small group at work (no more than four or five). For the best-quality tape recording, find them a space in a small office or storeroom near your classroom. They will perhaps need a couple of sessions to get used to the tape and may lark about with it or play up to it at first. But if you impose a strict rule that they must not switch it off or use the pause button, and if you give them positive feedback about the quality of their discussion, they will get used to it and will very likely improve.

Once you have a tape you can analyse it in a number of ways.

● Are they getting to grips with the task?
● What is the 'atmosphere' amongst them and why?
● Is the talk tentative/dogmatic/exploratory/polarised?
● Who is doing the talking and why?
● Who is getting squeezed out and why?
● Do different personalities make different kinds of contribution?

It may be very useful, though it will be very time-consuming, to make transcripts of key parts of the tape. This forces you to examine the talk minutely and will be very useful whether you intend to use the transcript with others or not. When you do make a transcript, leave wide margins down both sides for annotations. It may be possible to get one or two of the pupils involved to make transcripts for you – a salutary and educational experience for them, perhaps.

The outcome of such a close scrutiny should be kept clearly in mind. You need to be taken further along the road to answering the questions:

1 What kind of learning is going on here?
2 In what ways can I alter the context for the talk to improve the quality of the experience (for example, adjustments to: task; setting up; grouping; outcome)?

Devising supporting strategies

Teachers are pragmatic and inventive beings. They have to be to survive. Each classroom will have its own needs, problems and solutions. Teachers may well be able to take some relatively straightforward steps to encourage and support learning-talk in their individual environments. Amongst these may be:

● The provision of a talk-space either in or out of the classroom. Groups can 'book' this space as a better environment for discussion. Part of the classroom may be partitioned off with shelves. Perhaps a bit of carpet and some easy chairs can be conjured up.
● Built into all choice situations can be the option to take part in some talk work. This can be assessed as you would any other kind of work. Use talk for homework too (for example, interviewing adults, oral history, running commentary on TV programmes, recording ideas and opinions).
● Particular talk resources can be built up – for example, problems to be solved in groups, or specific pair exercises where one describes, say, a shape or map to another who draws it.
● The pupils could be encouraged to have their own cassette tapes which they store in school along with any other personal effects. Very cheap tapes could be bought in bulk for classroom use. During a year a particular pupil could gradually build up a collection of taped work in the same way as written work.
● You could make a point of commenting in detail on progress in talk on any report you make on pupils.
● To support your work in talk, you could use the extra help of older pupils or interested adults/parents in the classroom from time to time. It is very helpful simply having them around not only to *talk* to pupils, but to set up, service, keep an eye on talk work.

Departments or groups of teachers

The emphasis of my suggestions for work by individual teachers reveals my own bias towards teacher-led action research as a way of fostering personal development. This applies equally to the work of departments or related groups of teachers (for example, infant teachers in a large primary school – or the whole staff in a small school).

My suggestions for paired observations apply equally to departments. Groups of teachers are in a better position to carry out a more systematic and collective approach to the improvement of opportunities for learning-talk within their classrooms. Though individual teachers can work small miracles in their own classrooms, it is not sufficient that this little 'oasis' should exist merely for one year for particular pupils amidst a desert of past and future experience. Joint approaches and shared insights may lead to the offering of a more continuous and coherent learning experience for the pupil as he or she moves through the system.

Once a group of teachers has decided to take on board the issue of encouraging learning-talk in the classroom then the following suggestions could provide the basis for a rolling strategy. A kind of development is intended in the order below, but any single suggestion could in itself help teachers to go forward in their thinking. If adopted more-or-less complete I would imagine that the approach would encompass a year's in-service work.

Exploring philosophy and problems

Assuming the thrust for change has come at least in part from individuals, then particular teachers could introduce ideas to the department in order to lay the philosophical basis for change. It is essential that such theoretical explorations are firmly set in a background of practical realities. I have found it useful with teacher groups to follow up any philosophical sessions with one in which they are invited to 'brainstorm' together (felt tips and sugar paper?) all the difficulties and barriers for using classroom talk. At this stage it may be useful to refer to particular books or articles. The list of references at the end of this book only notes the books that have been referred to here and is not exhaustive.

Devising a strategy for change

Both teachers and pupils react more constructively where there is some kind of agreed purpose and outcome to their work. Creating an agenda or a timetable for any development work provides a framework for progress, a valuable focus for ideas and a positive pressure to move along with things rather than submit to the inertia of collective articulacy – the teacher's disease.

A programme of 'external' in-service work

I would recommend that during the early phase all teachers involved should attend an in-service course on a particular aspect of oracy, and follow that up with a presentation to colleagues. Where pairs of teachers can attend such courses together, the impact of follow-up and the impetus for change is more than doubled.

To keep 'course ideas' in context teachers could also visit other schools and classrooms doing interesting work in the area of oracy, or make contact with one of the number of interesting and innovative local and national projects which have oracy as their focus. The local Advisory Service should help here. The Wiltshire Oracy Project (Gilberts Hill Infants' School, Dixon Street, Swindon) has compiled a central register of people working on oracy-related projects.

Group enquiry into talk in classrooms

The teacher-led action research recommended earlier can be carried out within the context of the group strategy. It would be particularly valuable for a number of teachers to carry out a pupil-pursuit ready to report back and share impressions at the same meeting. The detailed examination of one or two transcripts of pupils working together is likely to have more impact than simply listening to a number of tapes superficially. If transcripts are presented with wide margins, teachers could annotate them individually before coming together to share ideas. The attention should centre on understanding what is going on in the talk on display: the process involved and the kind of learning that is evidently happening.

Learning workshops

Philosophical presentations can be too heavy; a programme of action-research too demanding or unwieldy. A more straightforward way – and one that can draw teachers into dialogue within a practical, experiential context – is to try out talk strategies with the group in a workshop situation. You would need more than four or five teachers to make it work, but the experience is a refreshing and enjoyable one which roots understanding of the learning experience firmly within the teachers themselves. In a small way, they are experiencing learning from the other end of the telescope. Try out a simple idea for about half an hour, then ask the teachers to reflect on the experience in 'diary' form for ten minutes. The discussion should then flow. This is an excellent way of fostering a felt awareness of the nature and process of talk for learning.

A document

I am uneasy about 'policies'. Language across the curriculum foundered in the late 1970s because too many schools imagined that once you had your language policy then you could put it in the filing cabinet and move on. Putting agreed practice down in writing does not ensure that the classroom experience of the learner is going to alter one jot.

But the process of producing some kind of statement of philosophy and practice as an outcome of doing work amongst a group of teachers can provide a valuable focus for discussions – a purpose towards which you are moving. Introduced at the right stage, the writing of such a document can serve to gel ideas and crystallise thoughts. Words exist at the sharp end of thinking and should not be confused with or substituted for the thinking process itself. When it *is* written, have a clear audience in mind as it could be useful in a wider context. Imagine you are writing for an interested if unenlightened parent – or for the most cynical and hard-bitten member of your staff.

Practical targets

Besides confirming the teachers' own commitment to making specific changes in classroom practice, discussions can bring more mundane matters into focus. Changes in rooms, timetables, extra equipment, furniture, staffing, will no doubt emerge as desirable, perhaps essential means of support for talk work. A group of teachers presenting a shopping list of reasonable and thought-through demands within the framework of a coherent policy for development may prove irresistible for a head, governors or LEA officer. Involve the head at a very early stage; keep him or her informed and invite him or her to your meetings.

Widening the circle

It is difficult to make any significant change in schools without in some way impinging on someone else's territory whether in a physical sense ('no, you can't hijack my store-cupboard') or a more philosophical one ('leave my learning model alone'). Sooner or later any group of teachers or individuals working for real change will come up against opposition or force choices between priorities that create 'an issue'. In this case it is wise for groups of teachers to take a 'whole-school' outlook from an early stage. You are working with other professionals in the same institution. The children meet the whole environment and a wide variety of its teachers daily. They are pretty good on the whole at adapting to the bewildering daily changes of differing expectations between teachers. There is no one more expert than they at working out what is in the overall hidden curriculum, no matter what the overt aims of individual enlightened or benighted teachers may be. The whole-school context profoundly affects your work and their experience, whether you like it or not, and whether you realise it or not. This is particularly true of the 'climate for talk' within the school. However individual teachers may seek to protect themselves from it, the ethos of the school will filter through to the learners and to the classroom and exert a pervasive and powerful influence in it.

This phenomenon has been charted by a number of notable recent books and reports. Boomer (1984, p. 117) says that language policies 'will be ineffectual unless they are accompanied by changes to the school's administrative structure, its curriculum and its educational philosophy' (p. 117). If we accept Boomer's premise in general terms, Rutter Report (1979) documents in some detail how the operations of the whole school context affects the learner in the classroom. HMI in DES (1980) stress here the importance to the perceived and hidden curriculum of 'the climate of relationships, attitudes, styles of behaviour and the general quality of life established in the school community as a whole' (p. 1). They were more specific in DES (1979, p. 100), where they report with some authority:

> Lessons in which the talk of pupils was directed towards learning occurred most frequently in schools where the general style took account of them as individuals and built on their experience inside and outside the classroom. Lively banter along corridors and, perhaps even more significant, the ease of silence between teachers and pupils, as well as – if too rarely – the personal talk in tutor periods at the start of the day, all contributed to the intellectual, social and affective significance of talking as a means of learning.

If we accept HMI's view in DES (1985b) that good learning is dependent on 'an atmosphere in the school which encourages children to respond in a positive and responsible fashion', then we can perhaps quantify this in terms of the personal relations in the school and the associated power structure. Of the former, Wells (1984, p. 12) concludes from his exhaustive study of the language development of individual children, that a crucially important factor in the development of talk is 'a warm responsiveness to the child's interest and a recognition of the child as an autonomous individual with valuable purposes and ways of seeing things'.

In the same volume Medway translates this into more political terms when he says 'acceptance of the need for expressive language implies a shift to a more equal distribution of power between teacher and taught' (p. 156). Holt (1964) puts this in a different way and begins to tackle the issue of teaching/learning models when he laments the stance that many teachers take which effectively blocks real learning: 'We present ourselves to children as if we were gods, all-knowing, all-powerful, always rational, always just, always right' (p. 169).

I am afraid to say that individual teachers, particularly those in big schools, may well be powerless to influence all this. Primary schools have a smaller-scale problem: they only need to get the right head and the changes in climate and ethos will quickly follow. A large secondary school is like a supertanker with its own momentum – a touch on the helm or a change of captain may do little to change its inexorable course and U-turns, if not impossible, take an inordinate time. The symptoms of a school which provides encouraging context for learning-talk would seem to be – warm and positive relationships among teachers and between teachers and pupils where everyone's contributions are valued, where dialogue and negotiation are part of the fabric of the place. In such a school there will be open structures for decision-making amongst staff and pupils will have access to these structures and to their own talk structures. There will be as much equality as possible and not much rank-pulling – so teachers may be on Christian-name terms with each other and rather than barking at pupils in corridors are more likely to be talking with them in classrooms, offices, staffrooms even. Teachers and pupils will have their freedoms restricted only in ways that make for the sensible, smooth and orderly running of a community. When pupils do wrong the emphasis will be on remedial action rather than revenge.

Teachers may be able to take small steps in alleviating some of these symptoms. But without recourse to a radical cure of the overall disease within the body of the school, there will be no significant improvement to its general state and the unspoken answers to the question of what learning is and of what school is for will remain unchanged. To influence the answer to these questions, schools need either a change of head, or a coherently expressed grassroots upsurge from teachers so powerful that even the least amenable head cannot choose to ignore it.

Given that your head may be there for some time yet, that grassroots upsurge can perhaps best start with the individual teachers and groups of teachers who alone or collectively embody parts of a school's climate for talk. If enough stones are dropped in the millpond then the ripples may eventually reach the shore. If groups of teachers have got themselves together about talk then at least they are in a position to try to influence whole-school thinking, even though it will undoubtedly be a whole-school task. The following could play a part in the process:

1 Involve your hierarchy. As I mentioned before, invite them to meetings, send them minutes, ask for their reactions. Try to interest an LEA officer in what you are doing (perhaps set up your talk work as a project, the results of which can be made available through the LEA to other schools). The introduction of school-focused INSET (in-service work) may well help here. Heads like LEAs to think good, exciting things are going on in schools. You may in this way get their overt support even if they remain unconvinced inside.

2 Try to 'book' some in-service time (whole-day conferences are obviously best) for whole-staff work. You'll need to have done your groundwork first and convinced key staff of the value of what you are doing. The workshop style of conducting actual lessons involving talk amongst teachers can again be valuable and a dynamic outside speaker with at least one foot in the classroom can help.

3 If you have indeed got the enthusiastic support of the school hierarchy and if they are prepared to pay more than just lipservice to the idea of talk as a central learning activity then they might be persuaded to establish a new, perhaps short-term, post in school to act as a cata-lyst/overview of the use of talk in learning. A ten per cent timetable reduction would release someone for the equivalent of a class (around four hours a week if you take marking and preparation into account). A responsibility post, even if temporary, would further enhance status and motivation. The teacher concerned would be given a wide-ranging role but might work from a specified brief and a framework of reporting,

preferably agreed by the whole staff. Besides disseminating good practice, producing evidence across the curriculum and publishing thoughts and accounts to the staff, the person could act in a number of new, stimulating roles: classroom researcher/observer; teaching in a pair with a teacher wishing to move forward; releasing other teachers for their own investigation. Such a post should best avoid labels such as 'language across the curriculum' which can vaguely be dismissed as 'English Department concerns' and focus more on *learning* strategies, with talk as the focus. Indeed I would wish heads to consider a number of such limited-brief positions, perhaps under the auspices of the senior post of Professional Tutor, Director of Studies or Learning Adviser.

4 It may be possible to establish within secondary schools an across-the-curriculum group of teachers and researchers enquiring into learning issues in their own classrooms. Such a group has the benefit of bringing together teachers from a variety of disciplines to discuss common issues, firmly based in the reality of day-to-day teaching and learning. Individuals from different areas may then go back and influence the work of colleagues in different ways. To avoid such a group becoming a clique it could work on a series of short-term investigations and present reports to staff before reconstituting for the next stage. In this way a healthy turnover is created as people leave or join the group.

5 One outcome of the work of such a group, or indeed of any department-based group, could be a document for the whole staff. Such a document could simply explain issues, present problems, raise questions rather than providing ready-made and easily resistible answers. Some teachers may also be appreciative of a more 'nitty-gritty' document, giving a number of practical ideas for approaches for using talk in the classroom. An example of one such document produced by teachers across the age and subject range in one family of schools is given in Appendix 2.

6 Luria said: 'Human mental development has its source in the verbal communication between child and adult'. Even if we find such a claim to be a little overstated, we can accept that contact with mature speakers is a key factor in the development of language. Given my earlier observations that teachers spend much of their interactive time amongst pupils on merely administrative exchanges (an observation supported by Wood *et al.* (1980)) then it would seem to be very important that teachers enable their pupils to have a greater variety of contacts with mature speakers both in and out of the classroom. This is best done as part of an agreed school policy and will certainly need the support of the head. A range of approaches to this is possible:

- Older pupils could spend time linked to a younger class. This would certainly be an important learning experience for them and may indeed link with any Humanities-based work they are engaged in elsewhere in the timetable. (I have seen a diary of experiences as a classroom 'auxiliary' offered as a successful piece of coursework.) In the case of sixth-formers intending to join any of the caring or teaching-related professions such experience would be invaluable. Older pupils could in fact begin by taking over some of the merely administrative tasks that so preoccupy teachers, releasing them for 'higher-order' tasks. In this way they could gradually gain the experience to take on more complex tasks. In the English Department I worked in during the 1970s we had a scheme whereby sixth-formers intending to go into teaching as a career were given the opportunity of a year's 'course' in classroom auxiliary work, which linked them firmly with a particular teacher and class, attempted to give them a theoretical grounding through timetabled seminars, and which provided them with a detailed testimonial, documenting their work and experience.

● It would, of course, be possible to encourage other adults into the classroom, both as occasional visitors, or as regular helpers. Be careful that the basis of such support is made clear. Like teachers, visiting adults are tempted to see themselves as experts transmitting knowledge to young minds. To help other adults to work successfully in your classrooms, you would do well to conduct one or two evening seminars to give them a grounding in the teaching model most appropriate to learning through talk.

Other adults could most usefully spend their time talking through work with individual children to offer them a chance to clarify ideas. It should be understood that any conversation which gives the children the chance to explain ideas in an extended way in a situation where they do most of the talking is invaluable, even if it is not directly relevant to the work in hand.

Indeed one can envisage a scheme, particularly in a primary school, where a number of enlightened adults are specifically available (and 'bookable' by individuals or groups of children) as discussion leaders. There has been much attention in recent years on schemes whereby writers-in-residence are attached to schools. Less commonly, artists of various kinds have been working in similar ways. There has even been a 'story-teller-in-residence' in one authority. So why not *talkers*-in-residence? You would not have to look for rare expertise or financial commitments. Communities surrounding schools are full of people who have the basic human interest and sympathy needed to offer children experience of extended contact with mature speakers even if it is simply at the level of providing an audience for the child's explanation of the story, painting, experiment they are engaged in. Home/school associations would be interested in the learning support such a scheme could offer, as an alternative to their preoccupation with fund-raising. I can envisage a situation whereby adults could work together in a team so that at all times someone is available as resource for talk. <u>Recently-retired people</u> might be particularly appropriate and the contact with the young would serve to build bridges in other ways.

- Older pupils will be able to go out to the community to gain such experience. Resulting links with old people's homes could be enormously valuable as could work-experience schemes and visits. All older pupils should have the right to arrange at least one day a half-term when they are visiting the wider community in some way. Even more valuable for some students would be a regularly timetabled school session whereby they joined an adult in the community in a support/learning capacity. Links with teenagers and parents with young children can be especially fruitful, as can those with older people living locally who perhaps cannot manage shopping or gardening. Put young people together with adults in these practical situations and the talk will arise naturally as part of the process of learning through human interaction.

And beyond

Schools are too frequently inward-looking organisations, concerned with their own private problems – though obvious public successes are noised abroad. There is a big world out there which we are all part of most of the time, when not cloistered in classrooms. The world is full of employers concerned that schools should turn out potentially successful employees. It is full of parents anxious that their children will succeed, though their criteria for success may differ from those of teachers. Governing bodies try to stand astride this school–outside world divide like a nervous and shifting colossus.

If parents, governors, employers and as many other adults out there as possible can understand more about what we are trying to do in schools then not only will our jobs be easier but we can perhaps begin to create a school/home/work continuity which will greatly enhance the development of our young people.

It is a mistake to feel that the concerns of teachers are poles apart from those of adults in the world outside. Schools are too fearful of consequences of opening up a genuine dialogue between teachers and other parties interested in education. On the surface there is a media-induced impression that schools are concerned to work in progressive ways to help young people to develop into thinking, caring citizens, whereas employers merely require literate, numerate, obedient servants, and parents simply want academic success. Some small-scale work that I was engaged in in 1986 challenges that view as does some recent research work in Wiltshire by Alan Howe (1983).

What importance do employers place on oracy? In a survey of 25 employers in Leicestershire varying from national corporations to those who employed only a dozen or so people I asked them what factors they considered most important when selecting young people for jobs. I asked them to give a one-to-five rating for each factor and the rank order came out as follows:

1 performance in an interview
2 appearance and manner
3 interests and relevant experience
4 quality of application letter
5 school reports and references
6 performance in their own tests
7 qualifications.

Twenty-four employers always used interviews in job selection and the others did so 'sometimes'. The bulk of them used a mixture of one-to-one interviewing and informal chat.

An important rider here is that several firms said that a certain standard of qualifications was needed before they would even consider interviewing people, but once that preliminary selection had been made, the qualification became the least important consideration. Indeed, it would appear that an articulate candidate would always have the edge over a less articulate but better-qualified candidate at this stage. Taking this still further, 20 out of 25 employers said that they would appoint someone 'with mediocre school reports and a very good interview' rather than someone else 'who is equal in all other respects but who has very good school reports and a mediocre interview'.

If this sample is in any way typical (and it is supported by the work done in Wiltshire referred to below) then it would seem to be clear that the employment chances of young people depend crucially on their ability to put themselves across in an interview rather than on paper qualifications. The same is, I believe, broadly true of Higher Education admissions, given a basic minimum of qualifications. But what form do these all-important interviews take, and what language demands do they make? Are they open and informal forums or merely the closed, one-way exchanges typical of so many secondary classrooms?

Employers said in the survey that the most important factors in the interviews were the answers of the candidates to 'more open questions where candidates are invited to express and develop ideas in a sustained way' and their 'ability to engage in discussion and exchange views'. Next, they felt that the 'ability to relate to the interviewer' was a key factor. Least important of all were 'answers to test questions to which there are right or wrong answers'. This is an enlightened set of responses, encouraging to any schools or teachers seeking to promote open and sustained discussion work.

To follow up these responses and to test their validity, I was allowed to sit in on a variety of interview situations involving school leavers so as to make my own observations. During these five interviews 88 questions were asked in all, an average of 18 per half-hour interview. This in itself is an interesting statistic. Even allowing for several minutes to get the candidates relaxed and sitting down, on average over a minute was spent on each question. This was not a reflection of the time the interviewers spent asking questions but an indication of the nature of the questions asked, and the expectation that the candidates should spend some time answering them. It was not uncommon for a candidate to spend upwards of two minutes over a particular answer, as compared to a few seconds taken over a straight-forward factual answer.

This would give clear credence to the low importance (revealed in the survey) of closed, test questions. There are a number of possible ways to categorise the 88 questions, but one relatively straightforward way to do this is to divide them into open questions, when the interviewer does not know the answer and there are a number of different possible answers (for example, 'Why do you want to be a receptionist?', and 'Tell us about your hobbies'), and closed questions, where the interviewer knows the answer and is in effect testing the candidate. An example of this kind of question would possibly be 'What tools would you need to . . . ?', but I cannot give an explicit example from the interviews simply because no closed questions were asked. It is evident that employers, in interviews, are seeking to draw out the candidates so that they can get an insight into their character, aptitudes and qualities, rather than test the fund of things they know.

A further way of categorising the questions would be to divide them into those which require an extended answer ('Tell us about your experience in the Scouts'), those that require a few words only in reply ('How long were you in the Cadets?'), and those which could be answered in any way the candidate thought fit ('What does your best friend think about you applying for this job?'). Analysed in this way, our 88 questions would sub-divide as follows:

Those requiring an extended answer	32
Those requiring a limited answer	38
Those requiring no implied length of answer	18

Many of the questions requiring limited answers were checking on details given in extended answers. For example, during an extended answer about how she worked at home a girl was asked: 'Do you always work with the radio on?' It was relatively rare for a 'limited answer' question to be an initiating or leading question and the 'extended answer' questions certainly held the key role.

Analysing the subject-matter rather than the style of questions is a little more difficult as a number of categories are possible and they tend to blur into each other. In general about two-thirds of the questions were to do with the self and the experience of the candidates and the remainder tended to explore career-related matters.

The interviews I sat in on were searching, rigorous occasions but they were conducted with a degree of friendly informality which encouraged the candidates not to be overawed, but to see themselves as equals within the discussion. Interviewers seemed concerned to relax the candidates and to draw them out in order to reveal the truest possible picture of their personalities. Commenting informally after the interview, employers confirmed this impression to me: 'We're looking for confidence ... bags of assurance ... We're looking for someone with personality ... you've got to put yourself across ...'.

How many of the thousands of lessons in their secondary school careers would have enabled these young people to develop these abilities, apparently so vital to their chance of obtaining a job? Two separate reports compiled in Wiltshire gave an insight into the kind of oracy demands made in the work-place once the hurdle of the interview has been successfully crossed. In D'Arcy (1983), having observed a number of work-places, noted a wide variety of demands on oral language, centring on the need for good communication and appropriate register. Employers stressed the importance of 'the ability to be articulate ... and the ability to ask intelligent questions'. Some employers commented on how much of the job was learned through talk and the value of 'powers of persuasion'. In a parallel report, Alan Howe (1983) stated how his research in a number of local firms helped him 'to recognize the view I had of much of industry as the stereotypical image it was'. He confirms the crucial importance of the interview in job selection and the key part that open-ended questions play. In his observations he noted the central part that talk plays in learning the job. At Marks and Spencer he concluded that 'the on-the-job training is all oral'. The Personnel Manager explained to him that 'Employees are expected to approach superiors. Their ability and willingness to ask questions is very important.' A selection of quotes from employees confirms this: 'Most of the communication here is by word of mouth' ... 'Problems are first talked about on the sales floor' ... 'relationships with superiors are much more informal than at school'. Howe stressed the need for schools to recognise that 'in adult life oracy matters' and concludes:

> If both the working environment and the adult world as a whole expect young people to be capable of coping with a complex variety of situations through talk, then schools need to examine carefully what they can do as a whole to provide pupils with appropriate contexts in which oracy can be valued (p. 13).

So far from being a limiting or deterministic influence on the school curriculum, I believe that the demands of the world of work could have a

wholly creative and liberating effect on the school curriculum. The emphasis, as D'Arcy (1983) writes, should be on the important processes of
'thinking, feeling, observing, verbalizing, doing – which school, shop floor,
office or Further Education share in common ... the threads which form
the fabric of so many aspects of our lives'.

When looked at in terms of the work-place, the school environment
would appear to be a very odd place indeed, and one which could learn so
much from the world of work. Handy (n.d.) says:

> What kind of workplace would it be where the workers had eight different
> bosses in one week in eight different work stations, often in groups of 35 or
> more, where they had no office, desk or phone to call their own, where the
> task was switched every 35 or 40 minutes, talking was often frowned upon
> and collaboration banned ...

Few of us would wish to work in such a place, and yet most secondary
schools operate in this way.

Schools have nothing to lose and everything to gain from opening up a
dialogue and partnership with the world of work. Such a creative relationship would have the potential to give great impetus to more progressive
views of teaching and learning in general, and to oracy in particular.

With that thought in mind, schools can confidently share with governors
and parents this common ground that I am convinced exists between the
'inside' and 'outside' world. Presented with the 'alternative' analysis given
above, few groups of adults interested in education could deny that talk
must play a central part in the learning of young people.

In a session with about 50 parents from the family of schools where I
worked on my action-research project in 1986, an enthusiastic consensus
was possible given the understanding the parents had of the importance of
talk in their own family and work situations. Common ground was reached
in considering 'practical' questions such as the two below:

1) You are living in a house with your wise and understanding uncle, who
   has books on every conceivable subject and plenty of writing paper.
   There are three things in your life you are trying to come to terms with
   at the moment:

   a) A particularly difficult tax form.
   b) The way your central heating system works.
   c) A crisis in your personal life.

   In each case would you prefer to tackle the problem by:

   Reading about it?
   Writing about it?
   Talking about it?

2) Your son or daughter has just left school with a reasonably good competence at reading, writing and talking. If somehow he or she could

become outstandingly good at one of these in later life, which would you wish it to be?

Recent quotations from the DES again were a source of comfort and enlightenment to those parents, even though they were from an Education Minister. 'In the majority of Primary and Middle schools there is over-concentration on practising basic skills in literacy and numeracy ... much work is too closely directed by the teacher and there is little chance for oral discussion' (Sir Keith Joseph in DES (1985a)). To reinforce to parents the messages about talk implicit in the starting-points offered above there is no more revealing, educative and refreshing method than conducting some lesson workshops amongst the parents, in which talk is the central activity.

In this section of the book I have argued that the theory of talk as developed in the last 20 years, though denied by everyday practice in schools, dovetails with the needs of society as a whole, including the world of work. Optimism must always overcome pessimism, and I *have* to believe that there is enough in common between these three apparently conflicting elements to ensure that talk-for-learning will eventually, perhaps sooner rather than later, assume its rightful place in schools.

A number of interests have emerged in the 1980s which, I believe, assist the cause of talk in schools. The Cockcroft Report (DES, 1982a) on the teaching of Mathematics advocated an emphasis on learning through talk. The National Association for the Teaching of English, a growing organ-isation, has long put forward a coherent view about the place of talk in schools. The equivalent Maths and Science teachers' associations now advance progressive viewpoints about learning through talk. Cross-subject movements such as the National Association for Primary Education, and the Campaign for the Advancement of State Education are beacons for the enlightened development of teaching and learning in schools. A State-funded initiative such as TRIST, TVEI, related in-service training, in its advocacy of active and collaborative learning approaches, has very much raised the status of talk. The Education for Capability movement, standing astride the worlds of work and education, has proved a powerful, well-publicised and influential force for good in education, and has consistently advocated talk as a means of learning and development. So the signs are good.

One of the most successful consumer movements in recent times has been CAMRA – the Campaign for Real Ale. Before its launch in the mid-1970s there was a distinct danger that full-flavoured, living organic beer could have been lost forever. It occurs to me now that what the equivalent movements in education share is a desire to promote *real learning* in schools as opposed to the currently more widespread (and commercially more viable?) gassy and tasteless variety. A coalition of forces in a 'Campaign for Real Learning' would prove a powerful, possibly irresistible influence, linking as it would with the tireless work of HMI and local authority advisers.

Until these forces can jointly and coherently impress themselves on the educational scene and support the pioneering work of individual teachers, departments and schools, then the gap between ideals and practice will remain unbridged. And until such time as teachers are moved to make a fundamental shift in their perceptions of teaching and learning then the story of talk will continue to be told fluently by academics but translated only in a confused and halting way into everyday classroom terms. The future of our schools as comprehensive institutions enabling the fullest range of young people to learn, develop and achieve their potentials is thereby on trial.

Appendix 1

THE GROBY ORACY RESEARCH PROJECT

This was in essence a school-based action-research project which I undertook on secondment during 1985–6 under the auspices of a Teacher Fellowship at Nottingham University. I offer an account of it here, not simply because it was the breeding ground for many of the insights contained in this book, but because I believe it presents a very useful model of research linked with teacher education.

In recent years there has been a rash of teacher-researchers liberated from normal school work by the creative use of the DES long-course in-service pool, linked to the need to shed staff due to falling roles. Revised funding schemes for LEA-based INSET (in-service work) that now operate will not favour longer-term, more expensive secondments. This is therefore an opportune time to offer a description and justification of a scheme such as the one I was involved in.

Schools have not always benefited from the presence of researching teachers in their midst. During my five years as deputy head of a large, progressively minded community school I and colleagues were the subject of substantial research on at least six occasions. On four occasions I was subjected to rigorous, structured, tape-recorded interviews by grey-suited men with clipboards who were unfailingly courteous but who only on one occasion provided any sort of feedback as to what they found out. Though their main area of interest appeared to be management rather than children in classrooms, the questions they asked were generally fascinating; some of the answers that eventually emerged from the research would have been more so, and might have enabled us to make our school a better place for young people to learn in. For that should surely be the major purpose of such generously-sponsored research activities: to make schools better places to learn in. As it was, I felt that the polite, grey-suited men were refreshing themselves and advancing their careers in a rather blinkered and parasitical way.

It was with these sorts of issues in mind that the Learning Group at Bosworth College (a self-help group of action-researchers) devised in 1982 a plan to try to combine the needs of researchers and schools. The idea was that members of the group could be seconded onto courses containing a large and open-ended research requirement which would enable them to work with teachers to develop mutual insights into children's learning and classroom practice. We discovered three such possibilities locally – MEd degrees by research at Birmingham and Leicester Universities, and Teacher Fellowships at Nottingham University. The first member of the group conducted his research in Birmingham in 1984–5. My opportunity came the following year.

Wanting to be completely liberated from exam demands, and having a congenital suspicion of certificates, I opted for the Nottingham-based Teacher Fellowship, which offered complete freedom to undertake a piece of research of interest to the LEA. What I wanted to do was to identify a general area that I thought would be of interest both to me, the LEA and to the schools, and to work jointly with a number of interested teachers on individual pieces of research that would be valuable in themselves and would contribute to a whole, coherent picture. The broad question I started with was 'How does the actual classroom experience of pupils across one family of schools compare with teachers' and educationalists' perceptions of how it should be?' In discussion with schools, my tutors and the LEA this base was then progressively narrowed; it focused eventually on one aspect: talk from five to 16. Following an 'advertisement' to teachers in the family of schools, 12 of them expressed an interest in becoming involved in some way in the research and I spent the first few weeks of the autumn term hammering out ideas for particular 'modules' of work to carry out with them in their own classrooms or interest areas. As these separate ideas were developed with individual teachers I tried to harness the burgeoning interest and provide some coherence to the project as a whole, by teasing out the main threads from the overall patchwork of research. These emerged as:

- What *contexts* (in terms of whole-school and particular classrooms and ways of working) would seem to encourage and facilitate such talk?
- What *constraints* hinder its development and use in the classroom?
- What *strategies* can be developed to enable such talk to happen?

Within these over-arching questions a number of pieces of research were completed. Much of the research fell naturally into two phases – an observation phase where I worked alongside the teachers as an auxiliary helper and observer, writing up ideas in diary form after the event. The diary was a shared one, open to the teachers who added in their own comments; some undertook their own observations, watching me teach their classes, or following a pupil for a day whilst I took their classes. We then reviewed our notes and ideas together to try to develop some new strategies for enabling talk to be used more effectively in an implementation phase.

Examples of research 'modules' to illustrate the style of working

In the primary school I was based in a final-year junior classroom and the observations centred on 'what kind of talk was evident there, and what other kinds of talk should be encouraged?' When the teacher and I reviewed the diary notes and matched our observations with recent reports and recommendations, we felt that the pupils perhaps needed more opportunities for extended discussion of ideas and for exploratory, tentative talk. We then set up sessions designed to encourage this which we team-taught and monitored together. The 'Campaign' work described in Chapter 9 was one outcome of this.

Two further examples of this kind of work are in the high school where I worked with a number of teachers on the theme of the comparison between what can be achieved in whole-class discussion and in smaller groups; and in the upper school where a learning support teacher and I tried to monitor the experience of talk of academically less successful students and devised alternative support strategies.

There were several other research modules at a tangent to the general theme of the use of talk, and at least two areas that frustratingly I felt unable to cope with, in a year when industrial action restricted my scope considerably. I would not recommend teacher-researchers to take on more than four or five projects in this way if they are to avoid some of the frantic plate-spinning activities and some of the short cuts I had to resort to.

It was of great value to allow particular ideas for research focuses to develop gradually rather than to have started (as with most conventional research) with a hypothesis that I was seeking to prove or disprove. With those kinds of blinkers you can miss seeing what is really important. Several of the pieces of research diverted significantly from the patterns originally discussed and agreed with teachers in the September. I believe that the flexibility to follow up the emerging interests and preoccupations of the teachers is the true strength of working in this way.

Working with and alongside the teachers gave me the companionship and intellectual stimulation that might otherwise have been lacking on such an open-ended course as a Teacher Fellowship. I had no formal lectures or course requirements, though I had full use of all the excellent facilities at the university and met at regular intervals with my two tutors who offered support and guidance. My seminars and lectures instead took place in staffrooms and pubs, over a coffee or a cheese sandwich and a pint. Somehow that was a more natural context for discussion and one which helped me to keep my feet firmly on the ground.

The more natural relationships created in this way with teachers in the schools concerned helped to lessen the 'threat' of an external researcher being present. Handbooks about research warned me to be careful about tactics and ethics. Never be seen alone with the head, I was told, and do not scrutinise the teacher between note-making. I would like to think that the more collaborative and supportive approach that characterised the project meant that such pits were not there to fall into in the first place. By negotiating the aims and methodology of the different research 'modules' with individual teachers, by working alongside them (and at times having *them* observe *me*) and by trying to establish a continuous and open dialogue about emerging findings, trust was built up so that the research was a source of interest to both parties rather than a threat to one.

The heads of the three schools whose unfailing support was a crucial element in any success had spoken enthusiastically in their evaluation of the project of the way that many of the teachers' interests and perceptions had been sharpened by involvement in the research. Their main concern was the dissemination of the work beyond those immediately involved. The seven research papers that were produced with the teachers as 'outcomes' from individual pieces of research were, of course, valuable in themselves, and were distributed to all interested members of staff. An example of one such paper is given in Appendix 2. They were used to feed ideas into debates already in progress and served to open up new areas of discussion. In the primary school the work fed directly into the creation of a language policy during the year of the research. Sessions were held with departments, governors and parents and classroom enquiry groups on the theme of oracy. In this way the work was not only a source of intellectual development and personal satisfaction for me, but it also helped the teachers and schools to inch forward in their perceptions of teaching and learning.

Had 1985–6 not been a year of traumatic industrial dispute I suspect that even more could have been achieved in terms of the active involvement of others. It seems to me that there is a way forward here that can marry the needs of theory and of practice, the researchers and the in-service needs of the schools, the theoreticians and the learners in the classroom they must surely serve.

Appendix 2

Below is an example of a pamphlet produced in co-operation with a number of teachers throughout the family of schools, as an outcome of the Groby Oracy Research Project, described in Appendix 1. Other papers were much lengthier and contained more detailed observations, but this particular one is interesting as it illustrates what ideas teachers at all stages share about the use of talk.

ENCOURAGING TALK

Preamble

This pamphlet aims to offer ideas for a richer and more consistent approach to talk across the age and subject range. Not all the points therefore apply with equal force and relevance to each particular stage or situation. We have tried to suggest practical strategies for overcoming difficulties and for encouraging effective and fruitful talk-for-learning. Though this is not a philosophical document, we invite you to share the following assumptions which have prompted us to write it:

1 Talk is a potent and natural means of learning, but in schools it tends to be overshadowed in importance by writing and reading.
2 To talk something through with others is an important way to grasp new ideas, understand concepts and to clarify your own feelings and perceptions about something.
3 A high proportion of classroom activity involves talk of two kinds: the teacher explaining while the pupils listen and answer the odd closed question; and pupils chattering in a non-purposeful way. This is not always disruptive, but neither is it fruitful.
4 It is important to encourage a more varied range of pupil talk in the

classroom where, for example, pupils have the opportunity to discuss ideas at length; explain concepts; describe; narrate; speculate; reason; instruct; work together on common tasks and problems; role-play.

5 Natural opportunities for such talk occur in a variety of subjects, activities and stages. The development of talk is therefore the responsibility of all teachers.

6 In adult life and in the world of work talk is far more important than reading or writing and makes increasingly complex demands on individuals. If schools neglect talk they will not only deny young people a vital means of learning but they will be failing to equip them for life.

Encouraging talk in your classroom

The climate for talk

1 The atmosphere should be a warm and understanding one where everyone's views are listened to and respected. Teachers will sometimes need to work hard to achieve this and if necessary deal firmly with pupils who cannot cope with it.

2 The teacher should avoid being the dominant expert. Pupils should do most of the talking and as far as possible be in the position of experts themselves. Teachers can often take a more fruitful role as listeners, tuning in to the talk of individuals and the talk going on in the classroom as a whole.

3 Talk must be a valued part of classroom activity and as such should be praised, commented on, assessed in the same way that we do with other modes of learning. Try to include talk-type opportunities in any choice situation and give it equal status with reading and writing. Why not talk for homework (e.g. talk with other adults to get their views, taped 'oral history', a taped running commentary on a sporting fixture on TV)?

Setting up talk opportunities

1 The pupils must be able to hear each other.

Small groups should cluster round one table. Three to five pupils works best. They should ideally know each other well but mates who mess about too much should be split up.

In *the whole class*, group the pupils round you at the front. An arrangement where an outer circle sits on tables and an inner circle on chairs can work well. Pupils can in this way talk directly with each other rather than through the teacher-as-megaphone.

2 *Prepare well for talk.* Just asking the pupils to talk about something is not necessarily very interesting and can invite failure. With all but those dream classes, you will need to stimulate their ideas first to get things going (A video? Something to read? Pictures? Jotting down first

thoughts? A demonstration? Some drama?). A way to improve pupil contributions in whole-class discussion is to ask them to sort out some preliminary ideas in small groups first.

Your aim must be to bring the matter for discussion to the front of their minds, to the very tips of their tongues. If you can succeed in doing this, the discussion will flow, whatever the context.

3 If appropriate, make arrangements for a taped or written record of a discussion. Tapes can be assessed and played back to groups for discussion. Small groups can be asked to jot down notes about their ideas and conclusions. For this it is sometimes best to have them all jotting things down on a common piece of sugar paper with a thick felt tip, rather than have a 'volunteer secretary'.

4 To encourage the purposeful use of talk in the classroom it will be clear from several of our suggestions that at least one, preferably two or three cassette players should be available for talk sessions. Portable cassettes with batteries offer more flexibility.

Criteria for talk tasks

1 The task or subject for discussion should be as *open* as possible, with scope for a variety of different responses. The aim should not be to arrive at the right answer, but to embark on a journey of exploration.

2 Therefore, you should not expect to encourage fruitful learning-talk for the pupils if the classroom talk consists of you explaining something they do not know about, and asking the odd closed question.

3 Try to start from where they are at – a position or situation they can cope with and have valid ideas about.

4 Discussions often work best if there is a purposeful outcome they are moving towards.

5 Giving tasks which lend themselves to polarised positions is more likely to lead to mindless argument than reasoned discussion.

6 In small groups, something *tangible*, a real object to focus on, is a powerful aid to discussion.

7 Fruitful discussion about the work in hand does *not* seem to take place if pupils are merely sitting together doing the same task separately. If you wish them to talk about the task, it is far better to have them working collaboratively on a common, shared task (e.g. writing or making something together).

8 Try to set up regular opportunities for individual pupils to talk one-to-one with a teacher or adult. For this you will need to involve other adults both in and out of the classroom.

9 If you use a set of questions for discussion, make them as varied as possible and sprinkle them liberally with open questions and ones where pupils can refer to their own experience. Pure comprehension questions

based on a piece of text rarely succeed in generating purposeful discussion.

10 It is a good idea to centre discussion on the pupils creating their own particular questions to ask about a certain text, concept or issue.

Some examples which have worked in this family of schools

In the primary school

1 Final-year juniors were asked to set up campaigns in groups aiming to get support for something to be changed. A great deal of intensive and extended discussion on issues was generated whilst pupils were trying to persuade others to wear their stick-on campaign badges.

2 Final-year juniors were asked to speculate in groups about what happens when a large can with some water boiling in the bottom was taken off the boil and sealed ... then they were asked to try to account for what actually happened.

3 Individual seven-year-olds were asked to create some fantastic Lego machines and then to explain to each other exactly how these worked and what they did.

4 A group of final-year infants were asked to describe all about human beings and life on Earth to an adult in role as a visitor from outer space.

In the secondary school

1 Third-years were asked, in groups, to select ten objects from a list of 15 that they would wish to have with them on a six-week stay on a deserted tropical island. Choices were then discussed in the whole group.

2 A fifth-year group was told some true-life creepy stories then jotted down ideas from their own experience, told them to each other and to the whole group.

3 A first-year Science group were given in small groups a pack of evidence to analyse as forensic scientists. They were then confronted by an adult in role-play as the lawyer of the accused who demanded precise accounts and explanations of their findings.

4 A Humanities group were asked to prepare and present a television news item on a natural disaster. The task involved some detailed research, and collaboration over diagrammatic and spoken presentations.

5 A small group in a World Studies class prepared for and conducted a detailed interview with the manager of a leisure complex. They also toured the complex making a running commentary on what they saw and their opinions about it. The work was presented solely on tape.

Appendix 3

THE IMPLICATIONS OF THIS BOOK FOR ORAL WORK AND
ITS ASSESSMENT AT 16+

> A civilized age of oral assessment awaits more civilized ways of teaching and
> learning.
>
> John Dixon

I welcome steps to include oral components in many GCSE syllabuses
across the curriculum. Yet the steps are but small, timid ones and the
stranglehold of writing and more 'respectable' modes of learning remains
firm. The national scheme of assessment for English serves as an obvious
example of this. Oral work is something separate, hived off from the main
body of written coursework upon which the final assessment is made.
Candidates merely have to achieve a minimum competence in oral work.
The status of talk in this kind of scheme is thereby diminished in comparison with many Mode III schemes previously operating which had
up to one-third of the possible marks for oral work. Indeed the present
scheme confines itself entirely to the assessment *of* talk. It makes no progress towards the assessment of overall language competence *through*
talk.

We must therefore regard present GCSE schemes as a half-hearted and
in some cases regressive staging-post for the continuing development of
the importance of oral work. I believe that the emphasis that is laid on oral
work across the curriculum, though understandably tentative given the
present state of knowledge, could and should lead to a rapid development
of knowledge about and good practice in oral work, providing oral work is
not approached in a deadening, mechanistic way. Given developments in
graded and staged assessment, progressive criteria and national curriculum,
the latter possibility is a very real danger.

This book has attempted to draw on past and recent thinking about oral work and has tried to assess how those ideas translate into the reality, on the ground, in the classroom. As such it has implications for the continuing development of oral work at GCSE level.

Firstly, it should be clear that the generation of successful oral work is not just a matter of the provision of new tasks in previous classroom and school contexts. The success of oral work depends crucially on the climate for learning within an individual school or classroom, and upon the learning model that exists within that classroom. Oral work will not thrive within the school or classroom where the overriding aim is the transfer of content. As I have argued, such classrooms encourage a depressing passivity and detachment amongst the learners. If oral work is to be more than the learners listening (or not) while the teacher talks then teachers must seek to create a more negotiative climate within the classroom where the learners are not only in more control of events, but can contribute to meanings and can shape and create their own within the offered parameters. The teacher must therefore be prepared to abdicate the inherited position of subject expert donating meanings and move towards the position of a learning expert, assisting the learners on the journey to their own solutions, their own meanings.

This in turn has whole-school implications. Such a teaching–learning model can thrive best and have credibility with learners (and their parents) if it exists not in isolation within certain subjects during the examination years, but across the curriculum and age range. We should not be having to convert pupils to the value of oral work during their mid-teens – a time when young people are understandably resistant to adult solutions. I see it as crucial that secondary schools and indeed families of schools develop a whole-school policy for talk which begins and operates from the moment the pupils enter that school. If such a policy is an enlightened and far-reaching one then schools should go some way towards breaking down the barriers between the primary and secondary approaches to learning, so that the transition becomes less of a grinding gear change and more of a natural flow between related experiences.

Such a policy will need the right climate of relationships within the classroom and school in order to thrive. Not only must individual teachers be better models of talking and listening than I judge them to be at present, but the whole school must consider ways of making itself a community of talkers and listeners. Unless there is the right combination of warmth and mutual respect amongst all participants in that community – between teacher and teacher, teacher and pupil, and between the pupils themselves – then fruitful learning-talk will not flourish.

Elsewhere in this book I have defined the nature of such talk and urged that teachers at all levels should direct their energies towards encouraging it. Hence my advocacy for a learning model that would encourage such talk. Approaches to GCSE must therefore nurture the development of talk that is more process-based and is less of a polished final product. Teachers are now beginning to see the value of pupils taking a more exploratory approach to writing, in which unformed first thoughts are valued both in themselves as committed engagements with the thinking process, and as stages towards more shaped and final products. Equally in oral work at GCSE level we should seek to encourage and develop this more tentative, exploratory kind of talk where the pupils are not so much *stating* understanding as *moving towards* it. It is vital, too, that we seek to assess this kind of talk as valuable in itself, and not as a first draft, to be thrown away once the final, fully-shaped version emerges. I firmly believe this is possible once teachers' minds and ears are fully educated about the value of such talk and about what it looks like when encountered. In Chapter 4 I tried to look carefully at the thought processes of pupils discussing an open-ended Science experiment. I advocated there that certain key scientific abilities and processes were clearly detectable (and hence assessable) within the expressive talk of the four boys concerned. In the same chapter a group of four girls in a discussion about handicapped babies reveal through their talk a sensitivity, imagination and empathy that, though it would be difficult to quantify, should certainly be taken into account in any assessment of their oral abilities. Indeed such talk could be regarded as more valuable than the more rehearsed and polished variety on show in the prepared talks of CSE orals in the past.

I would even be prepared to call exploratory, tentative talk a higher-order skill than the blunt expression of final understanding. Yet I would not wish to advocate a hierarchy of talking skills. The development of language is a much more organic, circular process than the neat stages of graded criteria, or benchmarks of achievements would have us believe. What is clear to me from my experience in schools is that language does not develop by a series of boltings on of abilities. Rather, development in language is more a question of the innate abilities being brought to the surface, of the unlocking of word-hoards. A mature and confident speaker, capable of complex sentences and of advanced vocabulary will not in one sense 'grow out of' more simple and childlike modes of expression. If he or she is to be a successful communicator he or she will retain the power of simple expression in his or her capabilities and use it when it is appropriate and effective – as when explaining something to a small child. It is the context of the language which is all important and should inform our judgement of its sophistication and effectiveness. Once language is taken in context it becomes communication. Communication in turn implies audience and hence our judgement of language ability should centre on the purpose of language and be governed not by notions of a hierarchy of skills, but by the yardsticks of appropriateness and effectiveness. We cannot therefore base our assessment of talk on the surface features of the language – the length of sentence or complexity of structure and vocabulary.

language use

We must instead attend to its contribution to the two-way flow of communication between people. In doing this we are in a sense making judgements on the speaker as a human being – we are assessing personal qualities as much as language ability. This is a much more challenging task for us, embracing as it does a holistic view of communication within a human relationship. Nevertheless this is an achievable goal. In the rest of this section I will attempt to be more specific about the means to this end.

The first thing to say is that there is no doubt in my mind that any assessment of oral work for exam purposes should as far as possible be part of the natural classroom activity. Until our ideas on the continuous assessment are fully thought through and until the ideas are supported by human, technical and in-service resources, we may have to rely as we have in the past on relatively formal and separate tests and assessment – orals rather than oral work – but in the long run we must seek to make our assessments part of the process of everyday teaching. For only if oral work is part of the natural, relatively relaxed flow of events will we be able to generate that expressive kind of talk – the sound of minds thinking and feeling – that is the most valuable talk for learning.

If we take that on board then we must ensure that the contexts for such talk are the right ones. I have already spoken above of the context of the whole school and the learning model. In Chapters 7 and 8 of this book I explored the more specific and immediate contexts for talk within the classroom. The messages from these chapters applicable to oral work and its assessment at GCSE level are clear – that the talk should be purposeful, open in nature, varied in its audience and purpose but having the main emphasis on talk between small groups of peers.

By 'purposeful' I mean that it should be part of a communication process which is genuine, or real enough to the participants to feel genuine at the time. In the past oral work for assessment has tended to be of the kind where a pupil has explained something to a questioning teacher who in reality knows more than the pupil about that subject. If we are to create purposeful channels of communication for the talk then we need to set up situations where meanings or knowledge need to be communicated and where such communication is a two-way process. So if we are, for example, to assess the candidate's understanding of aspects of Geography through talk, then we can arrange to have him or her talk with a group of younger pupils about, for example, glaciation. He or she can have maps and diagrams organised and can build in opportunities for questions and discussion. The teacher should ideally be present during this activity but the tape recorder can be used as a substitute monitor. In English Literature a small group could be set the task of devising a number of questions on a particular poem that will lead another group of pupils towards an understanding of it. In fulfilling this purposeful task of question-generating, the talk about the poem will flow. A further extension of this approach offering a different angle would be for the group to swap questions and poems with another group engaged on the same task.

In Chapter 9 I gave an example of role-play being used to generate talk in Science. Other subjects offer wide scope for such activity. History, with its emphasis on the understanding of human actions within historical contexts, affords particularly fruitful opportunities for such work. In role as a historical character a pupil could come face to face with other pupils, perhaps also in role, who ask probing questions. A controversial character could be put 'on trial' in the classroom. Besides the obvious 'product' experience of the trial itself, the 'process' experience of the lawyer, for example, rummaging through the historical evidence for angles on which to attack or defend the character on trial would provide a valuable opportunity to assess the skills necessary to a successful historian. Role-play can offer a rich variety of opportunities for talk which, though taking place on a slightly 'safer' ground than ultimate reality, are nevertheless sufficiently 'real' in emotional terms to generate an immediacy and motivation for talk than more everyday classroom situations. What all the examples I have given share is a degree of openness – in that the learner is expressing or working towards his or her own answers rather than being tested on answers which already exist in the teacher's consciousness. Without such freedom to participate in and contribute to classroom meanings, the talk will be inhibited in its response and restricted in its nature.

So teachers must be inventive and resourceful enough to devise a wide variety of mainly open contexts for talk so that what is assessed reflects the range of talk for learning appropriate in that subject. At least some of those contexts must give the opportunity for pupils to engage in what Gillian Brown (1984) calls 'long turns' – the chance for a more developed response where ideas are thought through and expressed more fully. Previously such opportunities have been afforded by one-to-one discussion between pupil and teacher – often in the circumstances of a formal 'oral'. I would argue that there is clearly a place in the teaching-learning process for such discussions, but for assessment purposes they are not only expensive in demands on the teacher's time, but restrictive in that the pupil is likely to defer expertise to the teacher and hence the flow of talk will be cramped. Teachers seeking to give pupils the opportunity for long turns would be advised to use other means: other adults within the classroom or community; the younger pupils referred to above; and for some pupils the use of the tape recorder 'solo'. My own experience of pupils working alone with a tape recorder is limited but I have seen some quite remarkable examples of pupils thinking things through and expressing their ideas alone on tape. This activity is an unusual and unnatural-seeming one and hence pupils will need to practise it and adjust to it. Within a whole-school policy that encouraged such work from an early stage it has every chance of becoming an invaluable classroom tool and a unique means of assessment of talk and of learning through talk.

I strongly believe, however, that the bread-and-butter of oral work and its assessment in the examination years should take place within small-group discussions between known and trusted peers. Throughout this book there are successful examples of such talk across the curriculum and age range. These examples show the following features: they involve a group of three to five peers who have learned to work together and hence have the background of a relationship of trust (if not solemnity); the matters for discussion are open in nature and have some kind of purpose or outcome; the pupils show a degree of commitment to the learning, either generated by the task itself or by their involvement with the agenda of learning. Teachers must therefore establish small-group work as a (if not *the*) natural classroom activity. The pupils must be aware of its value and share the teacher's desire to make it work. This can be best achieved within a whole-school approach to talk across the age range and curriculum.

If the pupils are to be inducted into the value of such talk and are to have a stake in its success, then I believe they must also be involved in its assessment. We take care to help the pupils to understand the shape that successful written work should take in our subject teaching. We may show them models of such work and take pains to go over difficulties they have with them. English teachers may point out features of spelling and sentence structure that make for surface improvements. We need to be equally painstaking in our approach to the evaluation of oral work and to the initiating of pupils into the criteria by which we judge its success.

Once we have done this then the way is clear to involve the pupils in the assessment process. At a very basic level they are already quite capable of keeping a detailed factual record or diary of their involvement in oral work which can run alongside a teacher's more detached assessment. If the pupils can also be involved in the critical evaluation of the work then not only will the teacher be able to gain a greater insight into the nature of their performance but the pupils themselves will learn and improve as a result of a greater understanding of the important factors in making a critical judgement about talk. The talk record/log/diary kept by the pupils can serve as an overall panorama of the oral work done; what else is needed is a series of 'snapshots' which afford the opportunity for in-depth study, and which can provide a sufficiently sound basis for moderation, evaluation and comparison to be reliably undertaken. The implication of this is that each pupil needs his or her own personal audio-cassette, in the same way that he or she has pencil, pens and ruler. Logistics may make it necessary for pupils to have a cassette for each subject in which oral work forms part of the assessment, but for the purpose of cross-curricular assessments there is some value in having all the talk in one place. There would be a particular problem when the work of several pupils in a group is recorded on a single cassette, but providing cassettes were carefully numbered and logged this is not an insurmountable hurdle.

To continue to explore the technical implications of the ideas expressed, it is also vital that each teacher involved in such work has at least one cassette player instantly available in the classroom. These are now such ubiquitous pieces of machinery that there is no longer a need to educate the pupils in the basics of their use, but it is well worth allowing them to experiment with groupings and sound levels for small-group talk. A general rule is to have the microphone central to a group of pupils and to have the volume a little below half-way. Built-in mikes are usually less clumsy and less distracting than separate mikes, though if you are aiming for studio-quality you will need more sophisticated equipment.

In this way it is possible to make reasonably effective and audible tapes within a normal classroom but I would strongly recommend that you designate an area, slightly detached from the everyday classroom, if you want better results. Perhaps a 'screen' could be created by arranging cupboards or bookshelves. You may even have a handy stock cupboard. Failing that you could scour the school for spare spaces – cloakrooms, corners, practice rooms, offices where a small group with a tape recorder could be accommodated. In my own school (supposedly an overcrowded one) a third-year group sent on such a mission with a map of the school on a Tuesday afternoon found 16 viable spaces (not including vacant offices), nine of which had sockets available. You will find that the number of spaces available for such work will roughly double if you are prepared to use batteries rather than search for that elusive electrical point. A creative use of space made available by falling rolls might be to designate a couple of small spare rooms as taping rooms, bookable for general use by a timetable on the door. A tape recorder might be permanently made available in such a room and the furniture could be set up for its use.

Given the ideal technical and physical resources, there are other, more fundamental implications for the working lives of the teachers involved. First and foremost, given the present undeveloped state of our under-standing and classroom practice concerning talk, it is essential that teachers work closely together to establish their own approach through a judicious blend of research and trial and error. Departments will need to educate themselves and share good practice. They will work far more effectively if this process takes place within the framework of a whole-school policy for talk, clearly understood by all.

If at all possible, the timetable should enable teachers to work together in subject or area-based teams. This will give them not only the opportunity to share expertise more directly but will facilitate more flexible approaches whereby different-sized groups could be created within a team-taught situation. If there is to be staffing enhancement as a consequence of the introduction of GCSE I would make a very strong plea that this be used not to make each class unit that much smaller, but to supply each subject discipline grouping with a support teacher as a bookable resource. This teacher should work in such a way as to reduce the *global* pupil–teacher ratio by working with smaller groups of pupils or by taking over the class of a teacher who is thereby released to undertake similar activities. Opportunities for this kind of work could be further enhanced by using the easily available source of interested adults in the community or older pupils to work with individuals or small groups in a purely facilitating way. There are schools, situations and classes in which it is a brave teacher who sends off a mixed bunch of teenage pupils to work totally independently without some avuncular figure to keep an eye on things and to help smooth over any difficulties.

The essence of what I have tried to argue in this Appendix is that we cannot expect success if we simply bolt oral work onto exam syllabuses without consequent changes in philosophy, pedagogy, organisation and practice. If teachers experience early failure in oral work because they have not been given the in-service background and physical support necessary to make such work successful, then we are in danger of ditching the inclusion of assessment of talk and assessment through talk in the first round of modifications to the new syllabuses. In that way we will have let slip through our hands a unique opportunity to make a shift in our classroom approaches – a shift which I believe could tip the scales in favour of the pupils and re-engage them in the power of the learning process.

References

References in the text cite the date of original publication. References listed hereunder follow the same convention, but page references in the text refer to the most easily accessible version of the work.

APU (1986). *Speaking and Listening: Assessment at Age 11*, London, HMSO.

Barnes, D. (1976). *From Communication to Curriculum*, Harmondsworth, Penguin.

Barnes, D., Britton, J. and Rosen, H. (1969). *Language, The Learner and the School*, Harmondsworth, Penguin.

Boomer, G. (1984). 'Negotiating the Curriculum', in Britton (1984).

Britton, J. (1970a). *Speech in the School, NATE Journal*, Summer 1965, pp. 22–24.

Britton, J. (1970b). *Language and Learning*, Harmondsworth, Penguin.

Britton, J. (ed.) (1984). *English Teaching: An International Exchange*, London, Heinemann.

Brown, G. (1984). *Teaching Talk*, Cambridge, Cambridge University Press.

Bulman, L. (1985). *Teaching Language and Study Skills in Secondary Science*, London, Heinemann.

D'Arcy, P. (1983). 'Language in Operation in Industry', paper published by Wiltshire County Council.

DES (1963). *Half Our Future* (the Newsom Report), London, HMSO.

DES (1975). *A Language for Life* (the Bullock Report), London, HMSO.

DES (1978). *Primary Education in England: A Survey by HM Inspectors of Schools*, London, HMSO.

DES (1979). *Aspects of Secondary Education in England*, London, HMSO.

DES (1981). *A View of the Curriculum*, London, HMSO.

DES (1982a). *Mathematics Counts* (the Cockcroft Report), London, HMSO.

DES (1982b). *Bullock Revisited*, London, HMSO.

DES (1985a). *Better Schools*, London, HMSO.

DES (1985b). *Education Observed: Good Teachers*, London, HMSO.

DES (1985c). *The Curriculum 5–16*, London, HMSO.

Dixon, J. (1967). *Growth Through English*, London, Oxford University Press

Donaldson, M. (1978). *Children's Minds*, Glasgow, William Collins.

Flanders, N. (1962). 'Using Interaction Analysis in the In-service Training of Teachers', *Journal of Experimental Education*, vol. 20, no. 4, pp. 313–16.

Froome, S. (1975). 'Note of Dissent' in DES (1975).

Galton, M. and Anning, J. (1986). Attitudes and the Infant Teacher, in *Child Education*, June 1986.

Gusdorf, G. (1965). *Speaking* (transl. Paul T. Brockleman), Evanston, Il., North Western University Press.

Handy, C. (n.d.). 'Organising for Capability', paper published by Education for Capability Committee.

Holt, J. (1964). *How Children Fail*, New York, Pitman.

Holt, J. (1967). *How Children Learn*, New York and London, Pitman.

Howe, A. (1983). 'Oracy in the Workplace', paper published by Wiltshire Oracy Project by Wiltshire County Council.

Illich, I. (1971). *Deschooling Society*, London, Calder and Boyars.

Martin, N., Williams, P., Wilding, J., Hemmings, S. and Medway, P. (1976). *Understanding Children Talking*, Harmondsworth, Penguin.

Medway, P. (1984). 'The Bible and the Vernacular: The Significance of Language across the Curriculum', in Britton (1984).

NATE (1976). *Language across the Curriculum: Guidelines for Schools*, London, Ward Lock.

Richmond, J. (ed.) (1983). *English in Schools: What Teachers Really Try to Do*, London, London Institute of Education.

Rutter, M. et al. (1979). *Fifteen Thousand Hours: secondary schools and their effects on children*, Open Books.

Tough, J. (1973). *Focus on Meaning*, London, Unwin Education.

Tough, J. (1979). *Talk for Teaching and Learning*, London, Ward Lock.

Watts, J. (1980). *Towards an Open School*, London, Longman.

Wells, G. (1984). 'Talking with Children: The Complementary Rules of Parents and Teachers', in Britton (1984).

Wells, G. (1985). *Language and Learning: An Interactional Perspective*, Brighton, Falmer Press.

Wells, G. and Wells, J. (1984). 'Talking and Learning', *NATE Journal*, Spring 1984, pp. 28–38.

Wood, D., Macmahon, L. and Cranstoun, Y. (1980). *Working With Under-fives*, London, Grant McIntyre.

Index

A Level examinations, 136
A.P.U., 27
action research, 3, 62, 144, 146, 150, 156, 159–62
active learning, 19, 133–4, 157
adults, use of in school, 144, 151, 165, 171, 174
Ancient Mariner, The, 7
Anning, J., 135
Aspects of Secondary Education in England, 26, 55, 82, 148
autonomy, 130, 136–7, 148

Barnes, D., 24, 25, 54, 60, 111, 125
Better Schools, 57, 157
Black Papers, The, 54
Boomer, G., 147
Bosworth College, 160
Brain of Britain, 78
Britton, J., 24, 33, 125
Brown, G., 142, 171
Bullock Report, The, see A Language for Life
Bullock Revisited, 55
Bulman, L., 27

CAMRA, 157
C.S.E. examinations, ix, 6, 169
Campaign for the Advancement of State Education, 157
'Campaign' project, 112–7, 119, 161, 166
Child Education, 135

Children's Choice, 138
Children's Minds, 13
Chomski, N., 13
classrooms,
    as environments for talk, 79
    atmospheres in, 99, 130, 164, 168
    furniture in, 79, 80, 98–9, 130, 139
    relationships in, 46, 87, 130, 168
Cockcroft Report, see Mathematics Counts
Cranstoun, Y., 56, 150
curiosity, 135
Curriculum 5–16, The, 27

D.E.S., 23, 24, 25, 26, 27, 51, 54, 55, 57, 66, 81, 82, 147, 148, 157, 159
D'Arcy, P., 155, 156
De Bono, E., 62
Deschooling Society, 14
Dixon, J., 24
Donaldson, M., 13
drafting,
    of oral stories, 35
    of writing through talk, 108–10

Education for Capability, 157
Education Observed: Good Teachers, 148
empathy, 49
employers, 110, 152–6
English in Schools: What Teachers Really Try to Do, 26, 28, 66
english talk in, 51, 52, 53, 104, 170

*English Teaching: An International
    Exchange*, 27, 50, 56, 147, 148
expressive talk, 24, 50, 55, 138, 139,
    169

Fifteen Thousand Hours (The Rutter
    Report), 4, 147
Flanders, N., 51, 54, 59, 60
Focus on Meaning, 24
From Communication to Curriculum, 25,
    111, 125
Froome, S., 23, 25

G.C.S.E. examinations, x, 83, 167–74
    passim
Galton, M., 135
geography, talk in, 170
Groby Oracy Research Project, 159–
    62, 163
Growth Through English, 24
Gusdorf, G., 24

H.M.I., 54, 57, 81, 91, 147, 148, 158
Half our Future, 23
Handy, C., 156
He-Man & The Masters of The
    Universe, 17
headteachers, 81, 115, 147, 148, 149,
    150, 162
Hemmings, S., 25
history, talk in, 6, 171
Holt, J., 13, 148
How Children Fail, 148
How Children Learn, 13
Howe, A., 152, 155
Hull, W., 13, 51
humanities, talk in, 60, 87–99 *passim*,
    104, 166

Illich, I., 14
infants, 14, 21
in-service education, 145, 149, 159, 162
interviews for jobs, 153–5

Joseph, Sir K., 57, 157
Journal of Experimental Education, 51,
    54, 59

language,
    acquisition of, 13
    modes of, 39
    register, 17, 21, 155
    scientific, 45–6, 121–5 *passim*
*Language Across the Curriculum:
    Guidelines for Schools*, 25
Language, the Learner and the School,
    24, 54, 60
Language and Learning, 24, 125
*Language and Learning: An
    Interactional Perspective*, 27
Language for Life, *A* (The Bullock
    Report), ix, 23, 24, 25, 51–4, 59,
    60, 66, 69
Language in Operation in Industry, 155,
    156
Lawrence, D. H., 3
learning logs/diaries, 50, 172
learning workshops, 146, 149
Leicester Mercury, The, 114, 116
long turns, 142, 171
Luria, A., 150

M. Ed. degree, 160
MacKenzie, R., 68
MacMahon, L., 56, 150
Martin, N., 25
Mastermind, 78
Mathematics Counts (The Cockcroft
    Report), 26, 157
media, influence of, 78
Medway, P., 25, 50, 148
Mode III examinations, 167
models of learning,
    interpretative, 111
    through the media, 78
    transmission, 78, 111
My Word, 19

NASA, 105
N.A.T.E., 22, 25, 157
National Association for Primary
    Education, 157
national curriculum, 167
National Oracy Project, x

O Level examinations, 83
older pupils, use of, 144, 150–1, 174
on-task chatter, 62–6, 67, 105

Piaget, J., 13
Primary Education in England, 54
primary schools, 52–4, 56, 58–9, 129–
    41 *passim*, 148, 161, 162, 166
pupil pursuits, 57–9, 142–3
pupils,
    as experts, 117–22 *passim*, 164
    attitudes to talk of, 69–77, 142

questions,
    closed, 48, 58, 59, 61, 154, 163
    from pupils, 58, 105, 107, 166, 170–1
    in interviews for jobs, 153–5
    open, 58, 102, 153–4, 165

racism, 88–97 *passim*, 136
relationships, whole school climate of,
    147–9
responsibility posts, 149–50
Richmond, J., 26, 28, 66
role-play, 20, 37, 104, 118, 121–2, 166,
    171
Rosen, H., 24, 54
Russell, B., 141
Rutter, M., 4, 147
Rutter Report, *see Fifteen Thousand
    Hours*

science,
    talk in, 6, 11–6, 121–5 *passim*, 166,
        169, 171
    thinking in, 45, 49
secondary schools, 52, 56–9 *passim*,
    129–41 *passim*, 148, 150, 166, 168
sexism, 17, 100–2 *passim*, 136
Space 1999, 17
Speaking, 24
*Speaking and Listening: Assessment at
    Age 11*, 27
Speech in the School, 24
Stenhouse, L., 125

storytelling, oral, 34–41, 117, 138, 166

TRIST, 157
TVEI, 157
talk,
    assessment of, 83, 167–74
    employer's attitude to, 152–6
    monitoring of, 83
    parent's attitudes to, 156–7
    policies for, 146–7, 150, 168, 171,
        172, 173
    pupil's attitudes to, 69–77, 142
    rationale for use of, 28
    teacher's attitudes to, 80–1
    whole school climate for, 147–9
talkers in residence, 151, 152
tape-recording, 14–5, 88, 143, 164, 171,
    173
Talk for Teaching and Learning, 26, 68
Teaching Talk, 171
*Teaching Language and Study Skills in
    Secondary Science*, 27
Teacher Fellowships, 159–61 *passim*
Times Education Supplement, 5
timetables, 139, 149, 173
Tough, J., 24, 26, 68
Towards an Open School, 26, 111
transcribing, 143, 146

Understanding Children Talking, 25
unlearning, 134–40

View of the Curriculum, A, 26

Watts, J., 26, 111
Wells, G., 27, 56, 82, 148
Wells, J., 56, 82
Whitfield, R., xi
Wilding, J., 25
Wilkinson, A., ix, 22
Williams, P., 25
Wiltshire Oracy Project, 8, 146
Wood, D., 56, 150
Working with Under-Fives, 56, 150
writing, relationship to talk, 37–41, 50